Windows® XP
FOR
DUMMIES®
QUICK REFERENCE
2ND EDITION

by Greg Harvey

WILEY

Wiley Publishing, Inc.

Windows® XP For Dummies® Quick Reference, 2nd Edition

Published by
Wiley Publishing, Inc.
111 River Street
Hoboken, NJ 07030-5774

Copyright © 2005 by Wiley Publishing, Inc., Indianapolis, Indiana

Published by Wiley Publishing, Inc., Indianapolis, Indiana

Published simultaneously in Canada

For general information on our other products and services or to obtain technical support, please contact our Customer Care Department within the U.S. at 800-762-2974, outside the U.S. at 317-572-3993, or fax 317-572-4002.

Wiley also publishes its books in a variety of electronic formats. Some content that appears in print may not be available in electronic books.

Library of Congress Control Number: 2004112333

ISBN: 0-7645-7464-7

Manufactured in the United States of America

10 9 8 7 6 5 4 3 2 1

2O/QW/RQ/QU/IN

About the Author

Greg Harvey, the author of more than 50 computer books, has had a long career of teaching business people the use of IBM PC, Windows, and Macintosh software application programs. From 1983 to 1988, he conducted hands-on computer software training for corporate business users with a variety of training companies (including his own, PC Teach). From 1988 to 1992, he taught university classes in Lotus 1-2-3 and Introduction to Database Management Technology (using dBASE) in the Department of Information Systems at Golden Gate University in San Francisco.

In mid-1993, Greg started a new multimedia publishing venture, Mind over Media, Inc. As a multimedia developer and computer book author, he hopes to enliven his future online computer books by making them into true interactive learning experiences that will vastly enrich and improve the training of users of all skill levels.

Dedication

To my alma mater, the University of Illinois at Urbana-Champaign, Illinois, birthplace of NCSA (National Center for Supercomputing Applications) Mosaic, the great-granddaddy of Microsoft Internet Explorer 6.

Thanks for helping me gain the analytical, language, and writing skills that all came into play in the creation of this work.

Author's Acknowledgments

Many thanks to Christopher Aiken at Mind over Media, Inc. for helping and supporting me with this revision of *Windows Quick Reference*.

I want to thank the following people at Wiley Publishing, Inc. as well who have worked so hard to make this book a reality: Tiffany Franklin for her help in getting this revision off the ground; Christine Berman for her tireless editorial assistance; and the amazing layout folks in Production. Thanks, too, to Kerwin McKenzie for the technical review.

Last, but never least, I want to acknowledge my indebtedness to Dan Gookin, whose vision, sardonic wit, and (sometimes) good humor produced *DOS For Dummies,* the "Mother" of all *For Dummies* books. Thanks for the inspiration and the book that made it all possible, Dan.

Greg Harvey

Point Reyes Station, California

Publisher's Acknowledgments

We're proud of this book; please send us your comments through our online registration form located at www.dummies.com/register/.

Some of the people who helped bring this book to market include the following:

Acquisitions, Editorial, and Media Development

Project Editor: Christine Berman

Acquisitions Editor: Tiffany Franklin

Copy Editor: Christine Berman

Technical Editor: Kerwin McKenzie

Editorial Manager: Carol Sheehan

Media Development Supervisor: Richard Graves

Editorial Assistant: Amanda Foxworth

Production

Project Coordinator: Maridee Ennis

Layout and Graphics: Andrea Dahl, Lauren Goddard, Jacque Roth, Julie Trippetti

Proofreaders: Laura Albert, John Greenough, TECHBOOKS Production Services

Indexer: TECHBOOKS Production Services

Publishing and Editorial for Technology Dummies

Richard Swadley, Vice President and Executive Group Publisher

Andy Cummings, Vice President and Publisher

Mary Bednarek, Executive Editorial Director

Mary C. Corder, Editorial Director

Publishing for Consumer Dummies

Diane Graves Steele, Vice President and Publisher

Joyce Pepple, Acquisitions Director

Composition Services

Gerry Fahey, Vice President of Production Services

Debbie Stailey, Director of Composition Services

Contents at a Glance

Table of Contents

Windows XP

This part gives you an overview of Windows XP by presenting some of the most common elements and introducing you to the kinds of things you'll most typically be doing with them. This overview covers three major areas: what you see in Windows, the basic procedures that you perform in Windows, and the typical kinds of projects that you can do with Windows.

The "What You See" section familiarizes you with four major Windows components: the Windows desktop (the place from which all the action takes place), the My Documents window (the window designed for holding the documents you generate), dialog boxes (specialized windows designed for making choices), and the Windows taskbar (the major Windows toolbar that usually remains present at all times).

The "Basics" section introduces the five most basic tasks with which all Windows users must be familiar. These include mundane stuff, such as opening and closing windows, creating and deleting files and folders, copying important files, and exiting Windows (and thereby shutting down your computer).

The "What You Can Do" section presents three projects that you may well want to undertake. The first project shows you how you customize the look and feel of your Windows XP desktop. The second project shows you how to copy music that you're playing in Windows Media Player into the My Music folder on your hard drive. The last project shows you how you can use the Windows Movie Maker accessory program to create both instructive and entertaining videos that you can play on your computer and easily share with colleagues, friends, and family.

In this part . . .

- ✔ What You See
- ✔ Taskbar Table
- ✔ The Basics
- ✔ What You Can Do

What You See: The Windows Desktop

The Windows desktop is the place from which you start and end your Windows work sessions. In the main area of the desktop, you see the background graphic, the Recycle Bin icon, plus icons for the shortcuts to your favorite programs and

Desktop icons

Start button

Quick Launch Toolbar: See Part I

folders and any Web items that you've downloaded. At the bottom of the desktop, you see the Windows taskbar with its Start button, Quick Launch toolbar, and Notification area. For more information on what you can do with these components, check out the appropriate *Quick Reference* entry in other parts of the book.

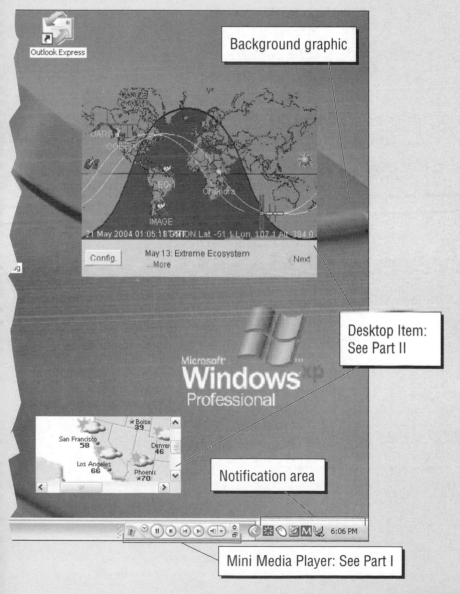

Background graphic

Desktop Item: See Part II

Notification area

Mini Media Player: See Part I

What You See: My Documents

The My Documents window shown in the following figure is typical of the windows you'll encounter throughout Windows XP. Note that this window is the default location for any files that you download from the Web or save in the Windows applications you use. This folder also automatically contains a My Pictures folder and a My Music folder, which are the respective default locations for all graphic and audio files that you save. For more information on what you can do with each of its components, check out the appropriate *Quick Reference* entry in other parts of the book.

What You See: Dialog Boxes

Dialog boxes come in several shapes and many colors (actually, they aren't a very colorful lot). Most of the dialog boxes you'll encounter (such as the Taskbar and Start Menu Properties and the Customize Start Menu dialog boxes shown in the figure that follows) enable you to select new options for the windows or programs that you have open. Dialog boxes contain a fair number of different types of controls, some of which present your choices in the form of text (entry) boxes or drop-down lists (boxes). Other controls include radio buttons (of which you can select only one in a group) and check boxes (of which you can select all or none in a group).

All dialog boxes offer some sort of command buttons for putting your choices into effect (usually in the form of an OK button) or opting out of any new choices (in the form of Cancel). The simplest of the dialog boxes (called alert dialog boxes) contain only command buttons (such as OK) that you use to acknowledge the message (often cryptic) that Windows has given you.

Many dialog boxes don't allow you to ignore them. This means that you must put them away before you can go back to work doing whatever you were doing. The easiest way to get rid of a dialog box (without putting into effect any changes you've made) is to press the Esc key.

For more on using dialog boxes in Windows XP, *see* the section "Dialog boxes" in Part I.

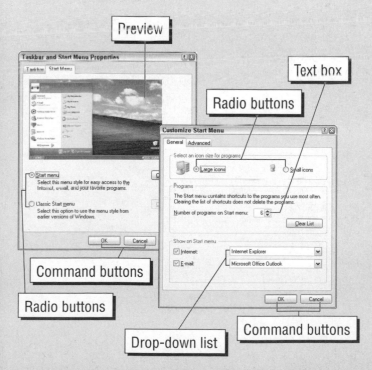

Preview

Text box

Radio buttons

Command buttons

Radio buttons

Drop-down list

Command buttons

BP-5

Taskbar Table

The Windows taskbar is far and away the most important toolbar that you'll encounter. The Windows taskbar remains present even when the rest of the Windows desktop is completely hidden by any full-size windows that you have open.

The most important button on the taskbar is the first one: Start. When you click Start, Windows opens the Start menu, which contains a number of important items, including

- **All Programs** to open a menu with the programs you normally use

- **Control Panel** to open the Control Panel window

- **Search** to open a menu for finding folders and files on your computer, searching the Internet, and finding people in your Windows address book

In addition to the Start button, the taskbar consists of the following three areas:

- The buttons on the Quick Launch toolbar that are used to quickly start up your favorite programs; *see* "The Quick Launch toolbar" in Part I for details.

- The area that shows all the minimized document and program windows that you have open; *see* "Switching between Programs" in Part I for more on these buttons.

- The area with the buttons that make up the Notification area; *see* "The Notification area" in Part I for details.

Tool/Button	Name	What You Can Do	Shortcut	See
start	Start	Open the Start menu	Ctrl+Esc or Windows Logo key	Part I
	Show Desktop	Minimize all open windows to display the Windows desktop		Part I
	Launch Internet Explorer Browser	Open Internet Explorer 6 and connect to the Internet		Part II
	Launch Outlook Express	Open Outlook Express so that you can send or receive e-mail		Part II
	Windows Media Player	Start Windows Media Player to play both local and streaming audio and video files		Part I
	Minimized window	Clicking a minimized window on the taskbar opens the window back up to its previous size		Part I

The Basics: Opening and Closing Windows

You can launch programs, open folders and files, or launch a shortcut from within a window or the Windows desktop by any of the following methods:

- Double-click the program, folder, file, or shortcut icon.

- Right-click the icon and then choose Open on its shortcut menu.

- Click the icon to select it and then press the Enter key.

For more on opening files and folders in Windows XP, *see* the section "Opening Files and Folders" in Part I.

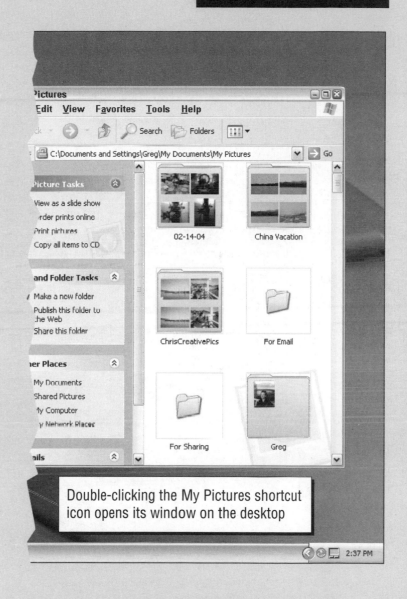

Double-clicking the My Pictures shortcut icon opens its window on the desktop

The Basics: Creating New Folders

You often might want to create a brand-new empty folder to hold the files that you're about to copy, move from elsewhere on your hard drive, or hold the programs you've installed. To create a new folder, follow these steps:

1. Double-click the My Documents or My Computer folder window from the Windows desktop.

2. Click the drive and then locate and click the folder on the drive that will hold the new folder you're about to create.

3. Click File➪New➪Folder on the window's menu bar.

4. Replace the temporary name "New Folder" with your own folder name and then press Enter.

For more on opening files and folders in Windows XP, *see* the section "Naming Files and Folders" in Part I.

The Basics: Deleting Folders and Files

The more you work with Windows, the more folders and files you'll create. Sooner or later, you'll probably have to delete some older ones or risk running out of hard drive space. To delete folders or files on a drive, select their icons and then choose among the following methods:

- ✔ Click the <u>Delete this Folder</u> hyperlink in the window's Info panel.

- ✔ Press the Delete key.

- ✔ Choose File⇨Delete on the window's pull-down menu.

- ✔ Right-click one of the selected icons and then choose Delete on the shortcut menu.

As soon as you use any of these three methods, Windows displays a Confirm Folder Delete or Confirm File Delete alert dialog box. Click Yes to send the selected icons to the Recycle Bin. Placing items in the Recycle Bin doesn't permanently delete them; to do that, you must clear the Recycle Bin. To clear your Recycle Bin (and actually reclaim the drive space used by the deleted items), open the Recycle Bin and then choose the Empty Recycle Bin button. Finally, click the Yes button in the Confirm Multiple File Delete dialog box to confirm the deletion.

For more on deleting stuff in Windows, *see* "Deleting Junk" in Part I.

Click this hyperlink to
empty the Recycle Bin

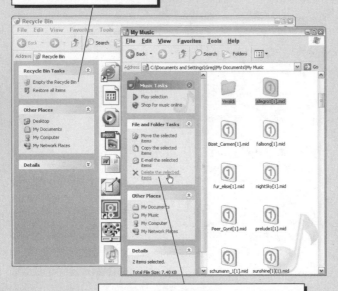

Click this hyperlink to send the
selected items to the Recycle Bin

The Basics: Copying or Moving Folders and Files

Windows XP offers a really easy method for moving or copying files to another drive or to another folder on the same drive; just follow these steps:

1. Open the My Documents or My Computer window and then locate and open the folder that holds the files and folders you want to copy or move.

2. Select all the files and folders you want to copy or move; *see* "Selecting Files and Folders" in Part I.

3. Click the Copy this File or Move this File hyperlink in the window's Info panel.

    Windows opens a Copy Items or Move Items dialog box (like the one shown in the figure that follows) where you select the (destination) folder to which you want the selected items copied or moved.

4. Click the folder to which the selected files or folders are to be copied or moved.

    Click the plus-sign buttons to display folders on particular drives and within other folders.

5. When the name of the folder to which you want the selected items copied or moved appears in the Folder text box, click OK to have Windows make the copies or do the moves.

For more on moving and copying files and folders, *see* the section "Copying (and Moving) Files and Folders" in Part I.

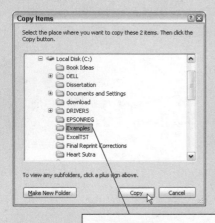

Select the folder to which the selected file(s) are to be moved or copied

The Basics: Exiting Windows

When you're finished working on your computer for the day, you should always shut down Windows by using the following procedure. That way, Windows has a chance to check your system's status before you power down your computer.

1. Click the Start button on the Windows taskbar and then click the Turn Off Computer button to open the Turn Off Computer dialog box (if you use the new XP Welcome screen logon) or the Shut Down Windows dialog box (if you use the Classic logon screen). *See* "User Accounts" in Part IV for information on how to switch between these two types of logons.

2. To completely shut down Windows and power down your computer, click the Turn Off button in the Turn Off Computer dialog box, or in the Shut Down Windows dialog box, make sure that Shut Down appears in the drop-down list box labeled "What do you want the computer to do?" Next, click the OK button or press Enter.

For more on the procedure of shutting down your computer, *see* the section "Shutting Down Windows" in Part I.

What You Can Do: Setting Up a Desktop Made to Order

My Documents • Investor • Microsoft ActiveSync • Questia - The Online Library of Books a... • Shortcut to IMGMGR.EXE

My Computer • Adobe Reader 6.0 • Roxio Easy Media Creator Home • WinZip • Wenlin

My Network Places • Dell Support • QuickTime Player • Microsoft Office Outlook 2003 • Microsoft Reade

Recycle Bin • iTunes • Shortcut to Dissertation • EndNote Program • Report a XP SP2 Bu

Internet Explorer • Windows Media Player • GuruNet • Microsoft Office Word 2003 • Site Transfers

Share-to-Web Upload Folder • McAfee Security Center • Solution Center • McAfee Scan for Viruses • AudibleManager

Adobe Acrobat 6.0 Professional • Napster • Microsoft Office Excel 2003 • Shortcut to CAPTURE.EXE • CDmage.exe

start

You can customize the Windows desktop in a number of ways.

1. Get started by:

Adding desktop shortcuts for the programs, folders, files, and Web pages you use all the time (**see** Part I)

Selecting one of the preset Windows color schemes or creating one of your own (**see** Part IV)

Adding shortcuts to programs that you use all the time to the Quick Launch toolbar (**see** Part I)

2. Work on your project by:

Adding desktop items (**see** Part II)

Arranging the desktop items on the Windows desktop (**see** Part II)

3. Add finishing touches by:

Selecting a background graphic either from a scanned image or a Web graphic you've downloaded from the Internet (**see** Part II)

Locking down the desktop (**see** Part II)

Creating a custom toolbar for the Windows taskbar (**see** Part I)

What You Can Do: Saving Music with Windows Media Player

You can use Windows Media Player to record and organize your music, as well as to play your favorite tunes. Windows Media Player in Windows XP makes it easy to copy music from audio CDs or from the Internet radio stations to which you listen. You can then organize the music that you copy onto the hard drive into playlists that you can play in Windows Media Player or copy onto portable devices, such as a portable MP3 player. If your computer has a CDR (CD recordable) or CDRW (CD rewritable) drive, you can even copy the music files onto blank CDs that you burn.

1. Get started by:

Marking the tracks on the audio CD you've loaded in the computer's CD player in the Copy from CD view for copying into the Media Library on your hard drive (*see* Part I)

Copying the tracks that you've marked into the Media Library of your computer or the song you're listening to on the Internet radio (*see* Part I)

2. Work on your project by:

Creating a new playlist for the music files you've copied into the Media Library on your computer (*see* Part I)

Adding specific music files to the playlist you've created in the Media Library (*see* Part I)

3. Add finishing touches by:

Copying the music files in your playlists onto your portable MP3 player or other portable device (*see* Part I)

Recording a new CD that you can play in any CD player with the music files in your playlists (*see* Part I)

What You Can Do: Producing Movies with Windows Movie Maker

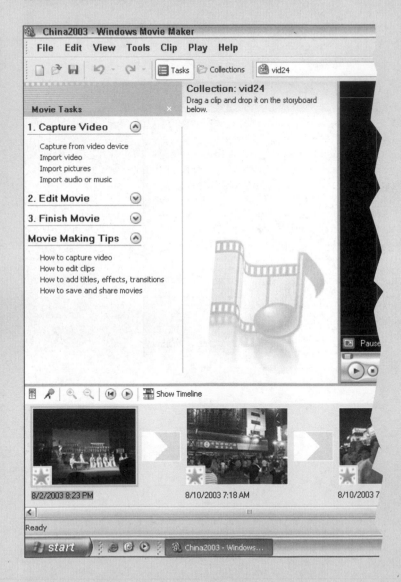

Windows Movie Maker is a new accessory that enables you to become your own movie director. You can take digital video, audio, and still graphics, and combine them into a movie that you can play (with the help of Windows Media Player) right on your computer. Windows makes it easy to send the movies that you create with Windows Movie Maker to your friends and family so that they can give thumbs up (or down) to your latest masterpiece.

1. Get started by:

Importing your video and sound clips into your movie project (*see* Part III)

Adding your video clips and still graphics in the Storyboard view (*see* Part III)

Adding your audio clips in the Timeline view (*see* Part III)

2. Work on your project by:

Editing the start and end points of the video clips (*see* Part III)

Synchronizing the sound track with the video (*see* Part III)

Previewing the final cuts of your movie in Windows Movie Maker (*see* Part III)

3. Add finishing touches by:

Saving the movie project as a movie that Windows Media Player can play (*see* Part III)

Playing the final movie on your computer with Windows Media Player (*see* Part III)

Sending the movie to colleagues, friends, and family as part of an e-mail message (*see* Part III)

Part I

Doing Everyday Stuff

Part I contains a pretty complete laundry list of all the essential "things to do" in Windows XP. You find out about such elementary stuff as controlling the icons on your desktop, adding and removing software and printers, regulating and dispensing with the files and folders that manage to clutter your hard drive, launching your programs, obtaining online help, and even safely shutting down the whole Windows kit and caboodle.

In this part . . .

Adding or Removing Programs

As you continue to use Windows XP, you'll undoubtedly get new programs that you need to install on your computer. Also, as time goes on, and disk space becomes more precious or newer versions of the software come your way, you may need to uninstall programs that you previously added. In addition to using Add or Remove Programs to install and uninstall application programs, you will use it to add and remove various Windows components.

Putting programs on your computer

To install a new application program from floppy disks or a CD-ROM by using the Add or Remove Programs Control Panel, follow these steps:

1. Click the Start button and then click Control Panel to open the Control Panel window.

2. Click the <u>Add or Remove Programs</u> hyperlink in Category view to open the Add or Remove Programs dialog box. If the Control Panel opens in Classic view (indicated by the individual icons rather than a list of categories), double-click the Add or Remove icon.

3. Put the CD-ROM in your computer's CD-ROM drive, or put the first disk in your computer's floppy disk drive.

4. Click the Add New Programs button on the left side of the dialog box and then select the CD or Floppy button to install a program from the CD or floppy disk you inserted into the drive.

5. Follow the steps outlined in the Install Program from Floppy or CD-ROM Installation wizard to install your new program.

You can also use the Run command on the Start menu to install a program from the Run dialog box. In the Open text box in the Run dialog box, type the drive letter that contains the disk or CD-ROM from which you're installing the program, followed by a colon and the name of the installation program (either **setup** or **install**). For example, to install a new CD-ROM game that uses <u>install</u> as the installation command, you type

```
d:\install
```

(assuming that D is the letter assigned to your CD-ROM drive; if this isn't the case, replace **d** with the letter your system uses) in the Open text box of the Run dialog box and then click the OK button or press Enter.

Use the Install Wizard to install all new Windows XP versions of software (also known as 32-bit versions of a program). Install programs from the Run dialog box when you install older software whose installation instructions talk about entering an install or setup command in the Run dialog box.

See also "Add or Remove Programs" in Part IV for more on using the Install Wizard.

Adding Windows Components

When you first install Windows XP (doing a standard installation), not all of the Windows accessories and auxiliary tools are installed, by any means. To install additional Windows components from the Add or Remove Programs dialog box, follow these steps:

1. Click the Add/Remove Windows Components button on the left side of the Add or Remove Programs dialog box to open the Windows Components Wizard.

2. In the Components list box, locate the category of the component(s) you want to add.

When the check box for a particular category is unchecked, that means that none of its components is installed. When the check box for a particular category is checked, but the check box is shaded (as opposed to white), this means that only some of the components in that category are currently installed.

3. To select which component(s) in that category to install, click the category icon or name to select it and then click the Details button at the bottom of the dialog box.

Windows displays a new dialog box, listing each of the individual components for the particular category. All those that are currently installed have their check boxes selected.

4. To install component(s) from the list, click the component check box.

5. After you're finished selecting components to install, click the OK button to close the dialog box and return to the Wizard Components Wizard dialog box.

6. Repeat Steps 2 through 5 for all the Windows components that you need to add. When you're finished selecting components to add, click the Next button to move to the next dialog box, where the wizard starts installing the selected components.

7. Click the Finish button when the Completing the Windows Components Wizard dialog box appears.

Be sure that you have the Windows XP CD-ROM in the CD-ROM drive so that Windows can find the files for the components you selected. Note that some components require that you restart Windows XP before their new settings take effect.

Taking programs off your computer

Windows XP includes an uninstall utility that takes the pain out
of removing unneeded or obsolete versions of a program from
your computer. To uninstall a program installed with Windows XP
(as I describe in the earlier section, "Putting programs on your
computer"), follow these steps:

1. Click the Start button and then click Control Panel to open the
   Control Panel window.

2. In the Category view, where you see a list of Control Panel categories, click the <u>Add or Remove Programs</u> hyperlink to open
   the Add or Remove Programs dialog box. In the Classic view,
   where you see individual Control Panel icons, double-click the
   Add or Remove Programs icon.

3. Click the Change or Remove Programs button on the left side
   of the Add or Remove dialog box to display the Currently
   Installed Programs list box.

4. In the Currently Installed Programs list box, click the program
   you want to remove (when you click a program name, the
   description expands to include a Change/Remove button or
   separate Change and Remove buttons).

5. Click the Change/Remove button or the Remove button, if
   Change and Remove are separate.

6. Click the OK button in the alert dialog box that appears to confirm your removal of the program. When the uninstaller finishes removing the program, click the Close button to close
   the Add or Remove Programs dialog box and to return to the
   Control Panel window.

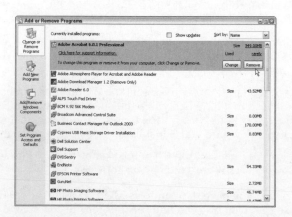

Use the Windows XP uninstaller to get rid of any unwanted program that you've installed with the Add or Remove Programs Control Panel. Using this utility to remove a program (rather than just deleting the program folder) ensures that all vestiges of the program are removed from the system and that you get back every byte of storage space to which you're entitled.

To remove unneeded Windows components, click the Add/Remove Windows Components button in the Add or Remove Programs dialog box and then locate and remove the check mark from the components you want removed before you select the Next button. Remember that if you remove the check mark from a category of components rather than from a particular component within that category, Windows will remove *all* the components.

Setting default Windows applications

New to the Add or Remove Programs window in the SP2 update to Windows XP is the Set Program Access and Defaults button. Click this button when you want to enable access to or change the default Web browsing, e-mail, media player, or instant messaging program, or to determine whether or not to use Microsoft Java Virtual Machine (abbreviated MSJVM, this is an extension of Microsoft's license to Sun Microsystem's Java source code that expires on December 31, 2007).

When you click the Set Program Access and Defaults button, the following categories, each with its own radio button and Expand button, appear:

- **Microsoft Windows** to use all Microsoft applications, including Microsoft Internet Explorer, Outlook Express, Windows Media Player, and Windows Messenger, no matter what programs you've installed

- **Non-Microsoft** to use all non-Microsoft Web, e-mail, media player, and instant messaging applications that you've installed on your computer

- **Custom** to select exactly which of the Web, e-mail, media player, and instant messaging applications installed on your computer to make the Windows XP defaults and to which to enable user access

To select a particular category to use, click its radio button. To display the actual list of applications used by each category, click its Expand button (the one with the two arrowheads, one on top of the other, pointing downward).

For the Custom category, to change default Web, e-mail, media player, and instant messaging applications and to determine which applications to grant access, click the radio button of the program you want to make the default, and click the check box to insert a checkmark for each program you want to be able to use by manually launching it from the Start menu or from a desktop shortcut.

Arranging and Sizing Icons in a Window

When browsing local files in any of three browsing windows (My Document, My Computer, and Internet Explorer 6), you can modify the size of the icons used to represent files and folders, as well as determine how much (if any) information about them is displayed.

To change the way icons appear in any of these windows, choose among the following commands on the window View pull-down menu. Note that the same menu options appear when you right-click in the window to display the shortcut menu or click the Views button on the window toolbar:

- **Thumbnails:** Changes the file and folder icons to little thumbnail sketches (each in a separate box). Use this option on folders that contain lots of graphics files, and you can use the thumbnail sketches to quickly locate the file or files that you want to use. Note that the My Pictures folder automatically selects this view.

- **Tiles (the default):** Displays the largest version of the folder and file icons, with their names to the right.

- **Icons:** Displays a smaller version of the folder and file icons, with their names below.

- **List:** Uses the smallest version of the folder and file icons, with their folders and filenames arranged in a single column along the left side of the window.

- **Details:** Adds columns of additional information (such as a description or the file type, file size, and so on) to the arrangement used when you select the List option.

Switch to the Icons viewing option when you need to see as much of the window contents as possible. Switch to the Details viewing option when you need to get as much information as possible about the files and folders in a window.

After you decide how file and folder icons appear in a window, you can also choose how they're arranged. Choose View⇨Arrange Icons By, and choose among the following options on the Arrange Icons submenu:

- **Name:** Sorts icons alphabetically by name.

- **Type:** Sorts icons by file type.

- **Size:** Sorts icons by size, from smallest to largest.

✔ **Modified:** Sorts icons by the date they were last modified, from oldest to most recent.

✔ **Show in Groups:** Arranges the file icons in groups by using the current arrange option (Name, Type, Size, or Modified) so that when Name is selected, files are put into letter groups, such as A, B, C, and so on. When Size is selected, the files are put into the following groups: Tiny (up to 50K), Small (51K to 100K), Medium (101K to 500K), and Large (above 500K).

✔ **Auto Arrange:** Arranges icons in columns by using the arrangement option in effect (Name, Type, Size, or Modified).

✔ **Align to Grid:** Keeps icons aligned by snapping them to the invisible desktop grid (note that this option is available only when arranging icons on the desktop — it remains dimmed in windows such as My Documents, My Computer, and Internet Explorer 6; *see* "Customizing the Desktop" later in this part for details).

The Name, Type, Size, and Modified options are not the only arrangement options you ever find on the View⇨Arrange Icons By submenu in the My Documents and My Computer windows. The additional options depend upon the particular drive or folder you have open in these two windows. For example, if you open the My Pictures folder in either of these windows, you also have access to an additional Picture Taken On and Dimensions arrangement option. If you open the My Music folder, you also have access to additional Artist, Album Title, Year, Track Number, and Duration arrangement options.

Browsing Drives, Folders, and Files on the Computer

You can't say that Windows XP doesn't give you sufficient ways to browse the components of your computer. In addition to the three major windows (My Documents, My Computer, and Windows Explorer) for browsing general stuff, such as local drives, folders, and files, you get a My Pictures window for browsing all the nifty graphics you scan, download, and otherwise cram on your hard drive. You also get a My Music folder for your favorite music clips. If you use the Windows Movie Maker to edit your video clips or download the Microsoft Reader to read your favorite electronic book online, Windows adds My Videos and My eBooks folders for storing your videos and eBooks as well.

My Documents

The My Documents folder provides a place to store your favorite files for easy and quick retrieval. This folder is often the default folder for saving the new files that you create with application programs, such as word processors and spreadsheets. The first time you open My Documents, the two folder icons, My Pictures (for storing your favorite graphic files) and My Music (for storing music files), appear. *See* "My Pictures" and "My Music," which follow, for details.

To open the My Documents folder from the Windows desktop, click the Start button on the Windows XP taskbar and then click My Documents at the top of the second column. To open My Documents from another folder, such as My Computer, click the Address bar drop-down button (on the right side) and then click My Documents at the top of the pop-up list (right below Desktop at the very top).

Note that Windows XP programs, such as WordPad and Paint, and Office XP programs, such as Word 2003 and Excel 2003, automatically save files to your My Documents folder unless you specifically choose another location. To save a file that you create with these programs in some other folder, you need to select that folder in the Save In drop-down list box of the Save As dialog box.

My Pictures

The My Pictures folder, located inside the My Documents folder, enables you to collect all your favorite graphics that you've scanned or taken with your digital camera (not to mention downloaded from the World Wide Web) and stores them in one easy-to-find place.

The My Pictures window automatically displays all the files in the thumbnail view so that you can tell what images it contains at a glance. However, the coolest thing about the My Pictures folder is that it also lets you browse through all the individual pictures in the My Pictures folder or in any subfolder within it by selecting View⇨Filmstrip on its menu bar. You can then advance through the images by clicking the Next Image button. To see the details in a particular image in the Image Preview window, double-click the thumbnail image in the filmstrip view or thumbnail view or the graphics file icon in the icon view. With the image displayed in the Image Preview window, you can do things such as:

- ✔ Zoom in or out on the graphic in the Image Preview window by clicking the Zoom In (the magnifier with the plus sign) or the Zoom Out (the magnifier with the minus sign).

- ✔ Print the selected graphic in the Image Preview window by clicking the Print button (the one with the printer) or by pressing Ctrl+P.

- ✔ Rotate the selected graphic in the Image Preview window clockwise by clicking the Rotate Clockwise button (Ctrl+K) or rotate it counterclockwise by clicking the Rotate Counter-clockwise button (Ctrl+L).

To open the My Pictures window from the Windows XP desktop, click the Start button and then click My Pictures (third from the top in the right-hand column in the Start menu). To open this folder from another folder, such as My Computer, click the Address bar drop-down button (on the right side) and then click My Documents at the top of the pop-up list (right below Desktop at the very top). You can then open My Pictures by double-clicking that icon in the My Documents window.

If your computer is equipped with a CD burner, you can copy all the pictures in the My Pictures folder or in a selected subfolder within it to a blank CD-ROM by clicking the Copy All Items to CD hyperlink in the Picture Tasks pane on the left (if the Folders task pane is displayed rather than Picture Tasks, click the Folders button on the My Pictures toolbar). Windows then opens a window for the blank CD-ROM, into which it copies thumbnails of all the pictures. Click the Write These Files to CD link in the CD Writing Tasks section of the navigation pane in this window to open the CD Writing Wizard, which takes you through the steps of copying all the files to a blank CD (assuming that they will all fit on a 650MB or 700MB CD).

Making slideshows

The navigation pane that appears on the left side of the My Pictures window contains a View as a Slideshow link that you can click to have Windows display your graphics files as a slideshow. When you click this link, Windows displays each of the graphics in the My Pictures window in succession for about 10 seconds at a time, starting with whatever graphic file is selected at the time. To control the pace of the slideshow or to pause or stop it, click the mouse button or press any key on your keyboard. Windows then displays a slideshow controller (with a group of buttons that look suspiciously like the ones on a VCR controller) in the upper-right corner of the screen. Here's how to use these buttons:

✔ **Pause Slideshow** (the one with the two vertical bars): Click to pause the slideshow.

✔ **Start Slideshow** (the first one with the right-pointing triangle): Click to restart the show.

✔ **Next Picture** (the one with the right-pointing triangle touching the vertical bar): Click to pause the show and advance to the next image in the My Pictures window.

✔ **Previous Picture** (the one with the left-pointing triangle touching the vertical bar): Click to pause the show and go back to the image you previously viewed.

✔ **Close the Window** (the red one with the X in it): Click to close the slideshow and return to the My Pictures folder on the desktop.

Note that after pausing the slideshow, you can advance to the next image by clicking the mouse button.

To close the slideshow and return to the My Pictures window, click the Close window button (the one with the X). You can also close up shop by pressing the Esc key at any time during the show, even if the slideshow controller isn't currently on-screen.

After you view a slideshow, Windows automatically creates a screen saver that is called (appropriately enough) My Pictures Slideshow by using the images in the slideshow. To select this screen saver and, perhaps, change the settings, use the options on the Screen Saver tab of the Display Properties dialog box; *see* "Display" in Part IV for details on changing these types of desktop settings.

Printing pictures

The navigation pane on the left side of the My Pictures window contains a link to the Photo Printing Wizard, which enables you to format and print your digital photographs. The Photo Printing Wizard automatically selects all the loose graphics filed in the My Pictures folder. To print photographs from a folder within the My Pictures folder, click the folder to select it before you click the <u>Print Pictures</u> link.

1. Click the <u>Print Pictures</u> link to open the Photo Printing Wizard and then select the Next button to move from the Welcome dialog box to the Photo Selection dialog box.

2. By default, all the photos in the My Pictures folder or the specific subfolder you selected prior to opening the wizard are selected for printing in this dialog box. To print just some of these photos, remove the check marks from all the ones you don't want to print. To remove check marks from individual photos, click those check boxes. To remove check marks from all the photos, click the Clear All button (you can then select the photos that you want to print by individually clicking those check boxes).

3. After selecting the photo to print, select the Next button to move to the Printing Options dialog box. Here, you can select a new printer to use (the Photo Printing Wizard automatically selects the Windows default printer) and/or a new paper size to use. To select a new printer, select it from the drop-down list box marked with the heading "What printer do you want to use?"

4. (Optional) To change the layout of the printing or the paper source, click the Printing Preferences button to open the Properties dialog box for your printer and then select the appropriate print options on the Paper/Quality tab or Layout tab (these tabs and their particular options vary according to the type of printer selected).

5. After changing your printing options, select the Next button to move from the Printing Options dialog box to the Layout Selection dialog box. This dialog box displays a list box of Available Layouts on the left, with a Print Preview box on the right. Select the most appropriate layout for printing the graphics on the designated paper size by clicking it in the Available Layouts list box. Then see how the photos will look using the selected layout in the Print Preview box on the right.

6. After selecting the layout to use, select the Next button to move the last dialog box of the Photo Printing Wizard, which shows you the progress of the photo printing. Note that you can click the Cancel Printing button in this dialog box at any time during the printing process if you run into some kind of printing problem that necessitates abandoning the photo printing.

If you don't have a printer suitable for printing your photos (perhaps you only have a black-and-white printer but want color prints), you can have them professionally printed by an Internet Print Ordering service. Select the photos to print or the graphic folder that contains them and then click the Order Prints Online hyperlink in the My Pictures navigation pane. Doing this opens the Online Print Ordering Wizard, where you can select the Internet printing company to use (such as Print⇨Fujicolor, Shutterfly, Yahoo Photos, or Kodak print services by Ofoto) and then specify the print size(s) and quantities. The Internet printing company you select then makes your digital prints by using its equipment and photo paper. The prices run from about $0.49 a print for a 4x6-inch print up to around $3.99 for an 8x10-inch print of a photo. The bill is charged to a credit card, and the prints are shipped to you via a courier service, such as FedEx, in a few business days.

My Music

The My Music folder is the place where Windows automatically saves all the audio clips you download from the Internet or save on your hard drive with Windows Media Player. The My Music folder, like My Pictures, is an automatic part of the My Documents folder.

To open the My Music folder from the Windows XP desktop, click the Start button and then click My Music (normally, fourth from the top in the right-hand column in the Start menu). To open this folder from another folder, such as My Computer, click the Address bar drop-down button (on the right side) and then click My Documents at the top of the pop-up list (right below Desktop at the very top). You can then open My Music by double-clicking that folder icon (the one with the music note in it) in the My Documents window.

Like the folders in My Pictures, the folders in My Music appear in thumbnail view. To play a particular audio file that you've saved in the My Music folder with Windows Media Player, right-click the file icon and then click Play on the shortcut menu. Windows Media Player opens and begins playing your selection (assuming that you haven't made another music player, such as iTunes or RealPlayer, the default).

To play all the audio files in a particular folder, click the folder icon before clicking the Play All hyperlink in the Music Tasks section of the My Music folder. To play all of the audio clips and tracks saved in the My Music folder, make sure that no folder or file is selected before you click the Play All hyperlink.

 Click the Shop for Music Online hyperlink in the Music Tasks section of the My Music folder navigation pane to look for new albums and videos online. When you click this link, Windows connects you to the MSN windowsmedia.com Web site. Once there, you can search for audio and video clips that you can download and play on Windows Media Player, and you can purchase your favorite audio CDs.

See also "Playing Music, Video, and Movies" later in this part for details on playing audio files with Windows Media Player.

My Videos

The My Videos folder is the place where Windows automatically saves all the video clips you download from the Internet or save on your hard drive with the Windows Movie Maker program. Windows automatically adds a My Videos folder to the My Documents folder on your hard drive as soon as you open the Windows Movie Maker program to view or save digital video clips on your hard drive.

To open My Videos from the Windows XP desktop, click the Start button and then click My Documents (normally, at the top in the right-hand column in the Start menu) before you double-click the My Videos folder icon. To open this folder from another folder, such as My Computer, click the Address bar drop-down button (on the right side) and then click My Documents at the top of the pop-up list (right below Desktop at the very top). You can then open My Videos by double-clicking that folder icon (the one with the film-strip in it) in the My Documents window.

Once the My Videos folder is open on your desktop, you can play any of the movies or video clips with Windows Media Player by double-clicking those file icons.

If your computer is equipped with a CD burner, you can copy all the video clips in the My Videos folder or in a selected subfolder within it to a blank CD-ROM by clicking the Copy All Items to CD hyperlink in the Video Tasks pane on the left. Windows then opens a window for the blank CD-ROM, into which it copies thumbnails of all the video clips. Click the Write These Files to CD link in the CD Writing Tasks section of the navigation pane in this window to open the CD Writing Wizard, which takes you through the steps of copying all the video files to a blank CD (assuming that they will all fit on a 650MB or 700MB CD, which well might not be the case, depending upon how long each of the clips is).

My eBooks

The eBooks folder is the place where Windows automatically saves all the eBooks that you download into the Library of the Microsoft Reader software from online booksellers, such as Barnes&Noble.com or Amazon.com. The Microsoft Reader automatically creates the eBooks folder in the My Documents folder when you download Reader. To access this folder, click the Start button and then click My Documents to open the My Documents folder. Then double-click the My eBooks icon.

The easiest way to obtain the Microsoft Reader software for your computer is to go to the www.microsoft.com/reader Web site or the eBook sections of the Amazon.com (www.amazon.com) or Powells.com Web sites and then click the Microsoft Reader hyperlink. The Microsoft Reader is a free download that takes about 35–45 minutes to download with a 56K modem and about 5–10 minutes with a DSL/cable modem.

After installing the Microsoft Reader on your hard drive, you need to activate the software so that it keeps track of the eBook titles that you purchase. (Many eBook titles have samplers that are available for free download. If you like the sampler, you can then later purchase and download the entire eBook.) After activating your copy of Microsoft Reader, you can then download a free copy of the Encarta Pocket Dictionary, which enables you to look up any word in the eBook text, and Microsoft's Text-to-Speech Package, which enables you to use the Book-to-Speech Package to listen to the text of your eBook titles with a synthetic speech engine.

The Microsoft Reader uses a special type called ClearType for rendering fonts so that they appear more legible on the computer screen and can be sized up or down as you want. It also enables you to annotate your eBook text with highlighting, notes, and bookmarks, which you can search from a special Annotations Index, and do a general search for any text. Best of all, Reader automatically keeps track of your place in the book so that you can always find your place in the text by using the <u>Most Recent Page</u> link.

Any eBook that you download for Microsoft Reader from an online bookseller is automatically placed in the My eBook folder on your computer. To begin reading the title, all you have to do is start Microsoft Reader and click the title name in the Library section.

You can use the Microsoft Reader to listen to audio books that you purchase and download from www.audible.com. Before you can listen to audible books by using the Microsoft Reader's Book-to-Speech feature, you must first install Audible's free audio management desktop software (available on its Web site) onto your PC. The Microsoft Reader supports Audible audio book formats 1, 2, and 3 (the higher the number, the better the sound and larger the file). Note that only Audible formats 2 and higher are playable on portable devices (see www.audible.com for the specific portable players supported). To play an Audible book after adding it to the Library of your Microsoft Reader, click the eBook's icon in the Library and then, when the title page appears with the audio playback controls at the bottom, click the Play button (the first one, with the triangle pointing to the right). You can then adjust the volume by dragging the volume slider and pause the audio at any time by clicking the Stop button (the one with the square icon).

My Computer

The My Computer window gives you quick access to the components of your computer system. To open the My Computer window, click the Start button on the Windows taskbar and then click My Computer on the right side of the Start menu.

When you first open the My Computer window, it displays all the major folders (including Shared Documents and My Documents), along with all local drives attached to your computer.

The My Computer window is very useful for getting an overview of the parts of your computer. To see what's on a drive or to open one of the folders in the My Computer window, simply open an icon as follows:

🖊 If you open a drive icon, such as a 3 ½ floppy (A:) or the hard drive (C:), or CD Drive (D:), Windows opens a new window showing the folders and files on that disk (note that the drive letters that appear depend upon the particulars of your system).

🖊 If you open a floppy drive that doesn't have a disk in it, Windows gives you an error message indicating that the drive isn't ready. If you meant to put a disk in the drive, do so and then click the Retry button or press Enter.

🖊 If the disk in the floppy drive isn't formatted, Windows displays an alert box, asking you whether you want to format the disk now. To format the disk, click the Yes button or press Enter to open the Format dialog box. *See* "Formatting a Disk" later in this part.

🖊 If you open a CD-ROM drive icon, and the drive contains an audio CD, Windows opens the Audio CD dialog box, which enables you to select the program that you want to use to play the CD (in most cases, Windows Media Player is selected by default). Click the icon for the program you want to use and then click OK to start playing the compact disc (*see* "Playing Music, Video, and Movies" later in this part for details). If the drive contains a cool game or some other data disk, Windows just opens a standard window showing the stuff on the CD-ROM. In the case of a game that you've never played, double-click the Install (sometimes called Setup) icon.

✔ To view the folders and files in your My Documents folder, double-click this folder icon.

✔ To search for a file or folder on your computer, click the Search button on the Standard Buttons toolbar to open the Search Companion Explorer bar. *See* "Searching for Files and Folders" in this part for details on searching.

✔ To use a Control Panel icon in the Control Panel window, click the <u>Control Panel</u> hyperlink in the My Computer navigation pane. *See* Part IV, "The Windows Control Panel."

If you prefer to have Windows XP open a separate window each time you open a folder or file icon in the My Computer window (instead of having Windows replace the contents of the My Computer window with the one you're opening), follow these steps:

1. In the My Computer window, choose Tools➪Folder Options to open the Folder Options dialog box.

2. In the Browse Folders section of the General Tab, select the Open Each Folder in Its Own Window radio button.

3. Click OK to close the Folder Options dialog box.

Using the Folders Explorer bar

Using the drive and folder icons in the My Computer window isn't the only way to explore the contents of your computer. You can also use the Folders Explorer bar to display the components of your computer system (including any network drives, if you use Windows XP on a network) in an outline view. This view of the My Documents window with the Folders Explorer bar displayed is known as the Windows Explorer in Windows XP.

To display (and hide) the Folders Explorer bar in the My Computer window, choose View➪Explorer Bar➪Folders or click the Folders button on the Standard Buttons toolbar. The Folders pane then appears to the immediate left of the navigation pane, listing all of the drives, both local and network, that make up your computer system.

You can also open the My Documents window with the Folders Explorer bar displayed by clicking the Start button on the Windows taskbar and then selecting All Programs➪Accessories➪Windows Explorer.

This list normally begins with the Desktop icon and ends with the Recycle Bin icon or Share-to-Web Upload Folder link, if you're on a network. In between these two, you see icons for My Computer and My Network Places (which you can use only if your computer is part of a network).

Of all these icons appearing in the Folder pane, some folders — such as the My Documents, My Computer icon, or My Network Places — may be expanded so that beneath them you can see icons representing the folders and documents within each folder.

Note the use of plus (+) and minus (–) buttons in the Folders list. When an icon has a plus button in front of it, this means that the level is condensed and that more sublevels are available with their own icons you can view. When a minus button precedes an icon, the level is currently expanded, and all icons on the next level are currently displayed.

To expand a condensed level, click that plus button. To collapse an expanded level, click the minus button. Note that when you click the plus button, it turns to a minus button at the same time that it expands the sublevels. Clicking the minus button turns it into a plus button at the time it collapses the sublevels and condenses the outline.

When the expanded folder/subfolder outline in the Folders pane becomes too large to view in its entirety, given the current size of the My Computer window, vertical and horizontal scroll bars appear as needed to help you navigate your way through the lists of folders and system components.

Note that you can resize the Folders pane within the My Computer window. To adjust the size of the Folders pane (relative to the other pane with the navigation pane and the contents area), position the mouse pointer on the dividing line between the two and then drag right or left when the pointer changes to a double-headed arrow.

To display the contents of a particular drive or folder on your computer system, expand the outline until that icon appears and then click the icon to display the subfolders and files in the contents area to the immediate right of the navigation pane.

Mapping network drives

If you use Windows XP on a local area network (LAN), and you save and open files in shared folders as part of a workgroup on a server, you can create a *virtual drive* (a special kind of shortcut to a folder on a network drive) whose drive letter appears in the My Computer window along with those of your local drives — a process referred to as *mapping a network drive*. To map a network drive, follow these steps:

1. Click Tools⇨Map Network Drive on the My Computer menu bar to open the Map Network Drive dialog box.

2. Click the Drive drop-down list button, and select the drive letter you want to assign to the virtual drive containing this network folder (note that the list starts with Z: and works backwards to B:) from the pop-up menu.

3. Type the path to the folder on the network drive in the Folder text box, or click the Browse button and select the folder directly from the outline of the network drives and folders shown in the Browse For Folder dialog box. (This outline has plus and minus buttons that work just like those in the Folders pane, which I explained in the previous section.) Now click OK to close the Browse For Folder dialog box and return to the Map Network Drive dialog box (where the path to the selected folder now appears).

4. If you want Windows to re-create this virtual drive designation for the selected network folder each time that you start and log on to your computer, leave the check mark in the Reconnect at Logon check box. If you only want to use this drive designation during the current work session, click the Reconnect at Logon check box to remove the check mark.

5. If you're mapping the network drive for someone else who uses a logon different from your own, click the <u>Different User Name</u>

hyperlink, and enter the user name and password in the associated text boxes in the Connect As dialog box before you click OK.

6. Click the Finish button in the Map Network Drive dialog box to close it and return to the My Computer window.

   The network folder that you mapped onto a virtual drive now appears at the bottom of the contents area under a new section called Network Drives, and Windows automatically opens the folder in a separate window.

After mapping a network folder onto a virtual drive, you can redisplay the contents in the My Computer window by double-clicking that drive icon.

To remove a virtual drive that you've mapped onto My Computer, click Tools⇨Disconnect Network Drive; next, click the letter of the virtual drive in the Disconnect Network Drives dialog box and then click OK. Windows then displays an alert dialog box, warning you that files and folders are currently open on the virtual drive and that you run the risk of losing data if files are open. If you're sure that you have no files open on that drive, click the Yes button to break the connection and remove the virtual drive from the My Computer window.

My Network Places

My Network Places (called the Network Neighborhood in earlier Windows versions) gives you an overview of all the workgroups or domains, computers, shared network folders, and shared resources (such as network printers) that are part of your Local Area Network (LAN). To open My Network Places from the Windows XP desktop, click the Start button on the Windows XP taskbar and then click My Network Places in the right-hand column of the Start menu.

To open My Network Places from another window, such as My Documents or My Computer, click the My Network Places hyperlink in the Other Places section of the navigation pane.

The following figure shows the icons in the My Network Places window that represent an entire network and the shared network folders.

The My Network Places can give you a graphic view of the domains and workgroups set up on your network and the resources that are networked together. When you first open the My Network Places window, Windows shows you all the shared folders to which you have access on the various networked computers.

You can display all of the networked printers and online faxes available to your computer by clicking the <u>Printers and Faxes</u> link in the Other Places section of the My Network Places navigation pane.

Network connections

In the standard LAN environment, your client computer is physically connected to the file server by cables connected to the network card and uses an Ethernet, Wireless Network, or other network protocol to make the connection. For other computers in the office that aren't equipped with network cards or computers that aren't physically located in the office, you need to create other types of network connections.

For example, if you have a computer that connects directly to another computer using a parallel or serial cable or that is equipped with an infrared port, you need to create a network connection for this type of direct linking. If you use a desktop computer at home and a laptop computer on the road (that needs to dial into the company's network), you would need to create a network connection for this kind of dial-up link.

To create a new network connection for your computer, you need to follow these steps:

1. Open the My Network Places window by clicking the Start button and then clicking My Network Places on the Start menu. (If My Network Places does not appear on the Start menu, access it by clicking the <u>My Network Places</u> hyperlink under

My Documents or My Computer. After you access it once or twice through one of these means, it should appear on the Start menu from now on.)

2. Click the <u>View Network Connections</u> hyperlink in the Network Tasks portion of the My Network Places navigation pane.

3. Click the <u>Create a New Connection</u> link in the Network Tasks portion of the Network Connections navigation pane to open the New Connection Wizard and then click the Next button to bypass the Welcome screen.

4. Select the radio button for the type of connection you want to create:

   • Connect to the Internet (to get connected to the Internet)

   • Connect to the Network at My Workplace (to dial into a company local area network)

   • Set Up a Home or Small Office Network (to connect to a small-office or home-office network)

   • Set Up an Advanced Connection (to connect directly to another computer using a parallel or serial cable or an infrared port, or to allow other computers to connect with your computer through the Internet, telephone line, or direct cable)

5. Click the Next button and then select the type of connection to create before clicking the Next button again.

   If you select the Connect to the Internet option, you can choose among Choose from a List of Internet Service Providers (ISPs), Set Up My Connection Manually, and Use the CD I Got from an ISP.

   If you select the Connect to the Network at My Workplace option, you have a choice between Dial-Up Connection and Virtual Private Network Connection.

   If you select the Advanced Connection option, you have a choice between Accept Incoming Connections and Connect Directly to Another Computer.

6. Specify the information on exactly how the new network connection is to be made. Depending upon the type of connection you're making, you may have to supply the telephone number to dial, the IP address to connect to, or the type of cable to use. After specifying the information required in order to connect (and for some types of connections, this requires specifying information in more than one dialog box), click the Next button.

7. In the Completing the Network Connection Wizard dialog box, enter the descriptive name you want to give the new network connection in the provided text box. To add a shortcut to this connection to your Windows desktop, click the Add a Shortcut to This Connection to My Desktop check box to add a check mark to it.

8. Click the Finish button to close the Network Connection Wizard and add the new network connection to the Network Connections portion of the My Network Places window.

9. Click the Close button in the Network Connections portion of the My Network Places window when you're ready to close the My Network Places window and return to the Windows desktop.

After creating a network connection, you can use it to get connected to your network or other computer by opening the My Network Places window, clicking the <u>View Network Connections</u> hyperlink in the navigation pane, and then double-clicking the connection icon.

 If you plan to use the network connection on a regular basis, be sure to click the Add a Shortcut to This Connection to My Desktop check box in the Network Connection Wizard's Completing the Network Connection Wizard dialog box. That way, you can always open a connection by simply double-clicking the connection shortcut on the Windows desktop.

If you're connecting to a wireless network, click the Wireless Network in Range link at the bottom of the Welcome to the New Connection Wizard dialog box; then select the network to connect to in the Wireless Network Connection dialog box before you click the Connect button.

Network Places

You can add shortcuts to the My Network Places window for any of the shared folders, Web share (special shared folders set up for Web servers running Microsoft Internet software), and FTP (File Transfer Protocol) sites to which you have access. To do this, follow these steps:

1. Open the My Network Places window by clicking the Start button on the Windows taskbar and then clicking My Network Places in the Start menu.

2. Click the <u>Add a Network Place</u> link at the top of the Network Tasks section of the My Network Places navigation pane to open the first dialog box of the Add Network Place Wizard and then click the Next button to move beyond the Welcome screen.

3. Make sure that Other Network Connection, Specify the Address of a Web Site, Network Location, or FTP Site is highlighted in the Service Providers list box and then click the Next button.

4. Type the location of the shared folder, Web share, or FTP site whose shortcut you want to add to the My Network Places window in the provided text box and then click the Next button.

   If you don't know how the blazes you go about doing this (each type of resource requires its own syntax: *server**share* for shared folders; http://*webserver*/*share* for Web shared folders; and ftp://ftp.*webaddress*.com for FTP sites), click the Browse button to locate and open the folder or FTP site in the Browse for Folder dialog box.

5. Type a common (descriptive) name that Windows assigns to this shortcut in the text box provided and then click the Next button.

6. In the Completing the Add Network Place Wizard dialog box, click the Finish button to close the wizard and open the shortcut. To close the wizard and return to the My Network Places window instead of opening the shortcut right away, click the Open This Network Place When I Click Finish check box to remove the check mark.

After creating a network shortcut with this wizard, Windows adds a folder icon representing it to the My Network Places window. To open the shared folder, Web share, or FTP site, you only have to double-click the folder icon after opening the My Network Places window.

Home Networking Wizard

Microsoft Windows XP supports home networking (in fact, this is the only type of networking that the Home Edition of the operating system supports). *Home networking* enables two or more home computers to share resources, such as a single printer, as well as allows the networked computers to share a single Internet connection.

To set up your home network (assuming that each computer is equipped with a network adapter that is connected with the appropriate cable), you can use the Home Networking Wizard to configure your network. To start the Home Networking Wizard, open the My Network Places window by clicking the Start button and then clicking My Network Places on the Start menu; then click the Set Up a Home or Small Office Network hyperlink in the Network Tasks section of the My Network Places navigation pane.

Although it is well beyond the scope of this book to give you detailed information on the ins and outs of setting up home networking, be aware that this wizard is full of hyperlinks that open Help dialog boxes that are full of good background information. For example, in the second Home Networking Wizard dialog box, you see a Checklist for Creating a Home Network link that, when you click it, displays a Help dialog box displaying a checklist of the steps you should follow in designing and setting up the network.

In addition to asking you questions about your computer and Internet connections, the Home Networking Wizard will check to make sure that your computer has the necessary Internet Connection Sharing software installed. (If not, you may need to have your Windows XP CD-ROM handy.) After you've used the wizard to set up your home network, you can use the My Network Places window as I describe in this section to check up on the shared resources.

Copying (and Moving) Files and Folders

Folder windows (such as My Documents and My Computer) are equipped with copy and move hyperlinks that appear in the navigation panes when you select one or more files or folders. These links, which appear in the File or Folder Tasks sections of the respective navigation panes, change depending upon what items you've selected:

- ✔ **Move This File** and **Copy This File** appear when you've selected a single file icon.

- ✔ **Move This Folder** and **Copy This Folder** appear when you've selected a single folder icon.

- ✔ **Move the Selected Items** and **Copy the Selected Items** appear when you've selected multiple files or folder icons.

To use these links to move or copy the file(s) or folder(s) you've selected, follow these steps:

1. Click the move or copy hyperlink in the File or Folder Tasks section of the window navigation pane to open the Move Items or Copy Items dialog box.

2. Use the outline of your computer components that appears in the main list box to select the folder where the selected files or folders are to be copied or moved. Click the plus-sign buttons to display folders on particular drives and within other folders.

3. When the name of the folder into which you want the selected items copied or moved is highlighted in the Move Items or Copy Items list box, click the Move or Copy button to have Windows make the copies or do the moves.

 Use the copy and move hyperlinks to copy or move selected items to new folders that don't yet exist on your computer. To create a new (destination) folder into which to make the copies or do the moves, select the drive or folder in which the new folder is to appear in the outline in the list box of the Move Items or Copy Items dialog box. Then click the Make New Folder button, type a name for the new folder, and press Enter. An icon for the newly created folder will appear in the outline, and you can then choose the Move or Copy button to have Windows copy or move the selected files to your new destination folder!

See also "Selecting Files and Folders" later in this part for information about selecting files and folders in a window.

Drag 'em up, drop 'em down

You can also copy and move files and folders to other folders on your computer by using the technique known as drag-and-drop. The art of drag-and-drop is simplicity itself and requires only that you do the following:

1. Select the object you want to copy or move. **See** "Selecting Files and Folders" later in this part for more on the techniques Windows XP provides for selecting objects with the mouse.

2. While continuing to hold down the mouse button, drag the object to a new location.

3. When you arrive at the desired location, release the mouse button to drop the object there.

To copy files with drag-and-drop, follow these steps:

1. Open the window that contains the items you want to copy, as well as the window with the folder or disk to which you want to copy the items.

2. Select all the items you want to copy. You can do this by drawing a bounding box around the file icons when they all fit into a rectangular shape: Click somewhere in the white space outside of the icons and then drag in such a way as to enclose all the icons in a box. As you drag, a bounding box made up of dotted lines appears, enclosing and selecting the icons within those boundaries.

3. Hold down the Ctrl key as you drag the selected items to the folder to which you want to copy them.

4. When the destination folder icon is selected (that is, becomes highlighted), drop the selected items by releasing the mouse button.

Note that when you drag files or folders from one drive to another, Windows XP automatically copies the files and folders, rather than moves them. This means that you don't have to hold down the Ctrl key when you intend to copy them from one disk to another. This also means that you must still delete them from their original disk after making the copies if you need to free up their disk space.

To use drag-and-drop to copy and move files, you need to have open both the folder with the files to be moved or copied and the one to which you intend to move or copy them. To help you in doing this, you need to set Windows so that each folder opens in a separate window. (Windows is preprogrammed to open each folder in the same window.) To do this, click Tools⇨Folder Options on the window menu bar, click the Open Each Folder in Its Own Window radio button on the General tab, and then click OK.

Drag-and-drop moving from folder to folder is great because it's really fast. This method does have a major drawback, however: It's pretty easy to drop your file icons into the wrong folder. Instead of panicking when you open what you thought was the destination folder and find that your files aren't there, locate them by using the Search feature; *see* "Searching for Files and Folders" later in this part.

Using cut-and-paste

Instead of turning to drag-and-drop, you can use the cut-and-paste method, the oldest way of moving and copying items in Windows. Cut-and-paste, as the name implies, involves two distinct processes. In the first, you cut or copy the selected files or folders to a special area of the computer memory known as the Windows Clipboard. In the second, you paste the item(s) saved on the Clipboard into the new file or folder.

You can perform the cut, copy, and paste commands, like many of the everyday tasks in Windows XP, by either selecting commands on the menu bar or by using keyboard combination shortcuts.

To move or copy files with cut-and-paste (using either method),
follow these steps:

1. Open the My Documents or My Computer window, and select
   the folder that holds the subfolders or files that you're moving
   or copying.

2. Select all the items to be copied and then click Edit⇨Copy (or
   press Ctrl+C) to copy them or click Edit⇨Cut or (press Ctrl+X)
   to move them.

3. In the My Documents or My Computer window, select the
   folder or disk to which you're moving or copying the selected
   folder or file items.

4. Click Edit⇨Paste on the My Documents or My Computer
   window menu bar (or press Ctrl+V) to paste them into the
   destination folder.

When using the cut-and-paste method to move or copy files or folders, keep in mind that you don't have to keep open the folder with
the files or folders you're moving or copying during the paste part
of the procedure. You can close this folder, open the folder to
which you're moving or copying them, and then do the paste command. Just be sure that you don't use the Edit⇨Copy or Edit⇨Cut
commands again in Windows XP until after you've pasted these
files and folders in their new location.

Note that if all you want to do is back up some files from your hard
drive to a floppy disk in drive A or B, you can do so with the Send
To command. After selecting the files to copy, just right-click to
open the shortcut menu attached to one of the file icons and then
choose the correct floppy drive, such as 3 ½ Floppy (A) or (B), on
the Send To menu. Oh, and one thing more: Don't forget to insert a
disk, preferably already formatted and ready to go, before you start
this little operation.

Creating New Files and Folders

You can create empty folders to hold your files and empty files to
hold new documents of a particular type right within Windows XP.

To create an empty folder, follow these steps:

1. Open the folder in the My Documents or My Computer window
   in which the new folder is to appear.

2. Choose File⇨New⇨Folder from the window menu bar or
   New⇨Folder on the window's shortcut menu.

3. Replace the temporary folder name (New Folder) by typing a
   name of your choosing and pressing Enter.

Creating a blank file

To create an empty file that holds a certain type of information, follow these steps:

1. Open the folder in the My Documents or My Computer window where the new file is required.

2. Choose File⇨New from the menu bar or New on the window shortcut menu.

3. Choose the type of file you want to create (such as Microsoft PowerPoint Presentation, Microsoft Excel Worksheet, Microsoft Word Document, Wave Sound, Text Document, or Briefcase, and so on) from the New submenu.

4. Replace the temporary filename (such as New Microsoft Word Document) by typing a name of your choosing and pressing Enter.

You can use your freshly created icon to open its associated program. *See* "Launching Programs" later in this part.

 Create a new folder when you need to have a new place to store your files and other folders. Create an empty file when you want to create an empty file in a particular folder before you put something in it.

Compressing files and folders

Short on disk space? You can now start conserving precious free space by creating compressed folders that automatically compress every file and folder that you put into it.

Windows XP handles file compression in two ways, depending upon what type of file system your computer uses. If your computer uses the older FAT (File Allocation Table) or FAT32 file system, you create a new special type of compressed folder so that all the files that you put in the folder are automatically compressed. If your computer uses the new NTFS (Windows NT File System) file system, you compress the folders and files after creating them; *see* "Compressing NTFS files and folders" later in this part for details on this method.

So how can you tell which file system your computer uses? Well, if your computer is a new purchase that came with Windows XP already installed on it, chances are very good that the manufacturer formatted your computer's hard drive using the NTFS file system. If, however, you upgraded from an earlier version of Windows, such as Windows 98 or Windows Millennium Edition, chances are pretty good that your system is using the FAT or FAT32 file system (FAT32 was an improvement to the system introduced in Windows 98 and supported by Windows Millennium Edition). If you upgraded to

Windows XP from Windows 95, I can guarantee that your system is using the FAT file system, because Windows 95 didn't support FAT 32 and NTFS.

However, you don't have to guess which system your computer is using, as there is an easy way to tell. Open the My Computer window by clicking Start and then clicking My Computer. Next, right-click the hard drive icon and then click Properties on the shortcut menu. The Properties dialog box that appears lists the file format (FAT, FAT32, or NTFS) on the General tab after the heading File System.

Compressing FAT files and folders

To create a blank compressed folder on a FAT or FAT32 file system, you follow these steps:

1. Open the folder in the My Computer window where you want the new compressed folder to be.

2. Choose File⇨New⇨Compressed Folder.

Windows creates a new folder icon (sporting a zipper to indicate its special zip-type compression abilities) that sports the temporary filename New Compressed (zipped) Folder.

3. Replace the temporary filename, New Compressed (zipped) Folder, by typing your own filename; then press Enter.

You can also create a new compressed folder on the Windows desktop by right-clicking the desktop and then choosing New⇨ Compressed Folder on the shortcut menu.

After creating a compressed folder, you can copy or move files and folders into it just as you would a regular file folder. As you copy or move files or folders, Windows XP compresses their contents. You can then copy compressed folders to removable media, such as floppy disks and zip drives. You can also attach them to e-mail messages that you send over the Internet.

Microsoft has even gone so far as to make the compression schemes that compressed folders use compatible with other compression programs. This means that you can send compressed folders to people who don't even use Windows (if you know any), and they can extract (decompress) their contents by using their favorite compression/ decompression program. Note that Windows XP automatically appends the name you give a compressed folder with the .ZIP file extension to help identify the folder as containing zipped-up files.

Program files that you place in compressed folders will run from right within them (simply by double-clicking its program icon), provided that the program doesn't depend upon any other files (such as those pesky .DLL files or some sort of data files). If the programs in the compressed folder do depend upon these kinds of auxiliary files, you must extract them before you can run the program. Also, be aware that when you open text or graphic documents stored in a compressed folder, they open in read-only mode. Before you or anyone else can edit such documents, they must be extracted from the folder. *See* "Extracting files from a compressed folder" later in this part for details.

Encrypting a compressed folder

When your compressed folder contains files of a sensitive nature, you may want to encrypt the files (the Microsoft term that simply means password-protecting them) so that only those to whom you entrust the password can open them.

Just be aware that you're out of luck if you encrypt the files in a compressed folder and then forget what password you assign. Keep in mind when assigning a password that it is case-sensitive (unlike Windows filenames), so it's not enough to remember just the letters in a password, should you decide to get fancy and use a combination of uppercase and lowercase.

With that in mind, you follow these steps to encrypt the files in a compressed folder:

1. Open the My Computer window with the compressed folder whose files you want to encrypt.

2. Double-click the compressed folder (remember, its icon should sport a zipper down the front) and then choose File➪Password on the window's pull-down menu to open the Encrypt dialog box.

3. Type your password in the Password text box, paying close attention to the case of each of the letters you enter.

4. Press the Tab key and then type the same password in the Confirm Password text box, exactly as you did in the Password text box above.

5. Click the OK button to assign the password to the compressed folder.

   If you don't replicate the password exactly, Windows displays an error message box, informing you that the New and Confirm passwords don't match. You must then click the OK button and match the passwords in the Password and Confirm Password text boxes by retyping the entry in the Confirm Password text box.

After encrypting the files in a compressed folder, each time you try to open any of them, the Password Needed dialog box appears; in it, you must correctly reproduce the password assigned to the files when encrypting the folder.

Note, however that even after you correctly supply the password in this dialog box, the selected file still opens in read-only mode (the only way to open them for editing is to extract — decompress — them from the folder). Note, too, that any files that you add to a compressed folder *after* encrypting it are NOT password-protected. To assign a password to such files, you must first decrypt the compressed folder (that is, remove the password) and then re-encrypt it.

To decrypt the encrypted files in a compressed folder, you follow these steps:

1. Open the My Computer window with the compressed folder whose files you want to decrypt.

2. Double-click the compressed folder (remember, its icon should sport a zipper down the front) and then choose File⇨Remove Password on the window's pull-down menu to open the Password Needed dialog box.

3. Enter the password assigned to the encrypted files in the Password text box and then click the OK button.

If you prefer, you can encrypt only particular files stored in a compressed folder. To do this, open the compressed folder in the browsing window and select the file (or files) to be encrypted. Next, choose the File⇨Add a Password command on the window pull-down menu, and enter the password for the selected file(s) in the Password and Confirm Password text boxes in the Encrypt dialog box.

It's hard enough remembering the password you assign to all the files in a compressed folder, let alone various passwords for individual files. If you go about assigning passwords to specific files, please, please be sure that you have a system (that you can remember) for which files get which password. Otherwise, you could have quite a nightmare on your hands when it comes time to open or extract the protected files.

Extracting files from a compressed folder

Because the files placed in a compressed folder automatically open in read-only mode, you may need to extract them (that is, decompress them) so that you can again edit their contents. To extract files from a compressed folder, you follow these steps:

1. Open the My Computer window with the compressed folder whose files you want to extract.

2. Select the compressed folder (remember, its icon should sport a zipper down the front) and then choose File⇨Extract All on the window's pull-down menu (or right-click the folder icon and choose Extract on its shortcut menu) to open the first dialog box of the Extract Wizard.

3. Replace the path and the filename of the compressed folder with the pathname of the folder in which you want to store the extracted (decompressed) files in the text box labeled "Files will be extracted to this directory."

   To browse to the folder in which you want the extracted files copied, click the Browse button; then select the (destination) folder in the outline of your computer system, and click OK. To extract the files in their original compressed folder, don't replace the path and filename for the compressed folder that appear in this text box. Just be aware that the only way to recompress the files that you extract in the compressed folder is to first move them out of the folder and then move them back in!

4. (Optional) If the compressed folder contains encrypted files that use the same password, and you want to extract them all, click the Password button (immediately below the Browse button) and then type the password in the next text box that appears.

   Note that if the compressed folder contains encrypted files that use different passwords, or if you don't want all the encrypted files to be extracted, don't click the Password button in Step 4. Instead, go on to Step 5, and click the Next button. After you click this button, a Password Needed dialog box appears for the first encrypted file in the folder. Enter the file password in the Password text box and choose OK, or click the Skip File button if you want to bypass the extraction of that file (or if you just can't come up with the correct password).

5. Click the Next button at the bottom of the first Extract Wizard dialog box to begin extracting the files.

   As soon as Windows finishes extracting the files, the second Extract Wizard dialog box appears.

6. (Optional) If you want to have Windows open the folder with the extracted files right after you close the Extract Wizard, select the Show extracted files check box.

7. Click the Finish button to close the Extract Wizard dialog box.

To extract only particular files from a compressed folder, open the compressed folder in one of the browsing windows, select the file or files to be extracted, and then choose the File⇨Extract command on the window pull-down menu.

See also "Naming Files and Folders" later in this part for information on naming new files and folders in Windows XP.

Compressing NTFS files and folders

To compress files and folders on a system that uses the NTFS file system, follow these steps:

1. Select the folder or file that you want to compress in the My Documents, Windows Explorer, or My Computer window.

2. Right-click the folder or file icon and then click Properties at the end of the shortcut menu to open the Properties dialog box for the selected file or folder.

3. Click the Advanced button to open the Advanced Attributes dialog box.

4. Click the Compress Contents to Save Disk Space check box and then click OK to close the Advanced Attributes dialog box.

5. If you're compressing a folder, an alert box asking you to confirm your attribute changes appears, with the Apply Changes to This Folder, Subfolders, and Files Only radio button selected. If you want to compress only the selected folder without affecting its subfolders and their files as well, click the Apply Changes to This Folder Only radio button before you click OK.

6. Click the Close button in the My Documents and My Computer windows to return to the Windows desktop.

Note that if you compress a folder, all the files in that folder are compressed. Any new files that you place in the folder after compressing it are likewise automatically compressed.

Note that you can encrypt NTFS files and folders to secure your files by selecting the Encrypt Contents to Secure Data check box in the Advanced Attributes dialog box. However, selecting this encryption check box automatically deselects the Compress Contents to Save Disk Space check box — you can't both compress and encrypt a folder or file at the same time.

When you encrypt a folder, Windows displays an alert dialog box asking if you want to encrypt all of the subfolders and folders within it. Likewise, when you encrypt a single file, you receive an alert dialog box asking if you want to encrypt not only the file, but the parent folder as well.

When you encrypt a folder, all the files that you subsequently put into that folder are automatically encrypted. If, however, you move an encrypted file into an unencrypted folder, Windows removes the file encryption.

Sharing folders on a network

You can share your folders and files across the same network or share them on the Internet by publishing them to the Web (*see* Part II for details). To share a folder and all the file it contains on the same network, you follow these steps:

1. Open Windows Explorer by double-clicking the My Computer icon on the desktop and then clicking the Folders button on the Standard Buttons toolbar (or right-click the Start button and then choose Explore on the shortcut menu).

2. Select the folder in the Folders pane before you right-click the icon of the folder you want to share in the right side of the window and then click the Sharing and Security item at the bottom of its shortcut menu.

3. Make sure the Sharing tab in the Folder's Properties dialog box is selected and then click the <u>Shared Documents</u> link in the description "To share this folder with other users on this computer, drag it to the Shared Documents folder."

   Windows then opens the Shared Documents window, overlapping the Windows Explorer window.

4. Drag the folder icon from the Windows Explorer window, and drop in the Shared Documents window.

After you move a folder to the Shared Documents window, all the network users who have access to your computer can use its files by opening Shared Documents folder on your computer (the path to which is C:\Documents and Settings\All Users\Shared Documents).

Creating Shortcuts

Shortcuts make it possible to open an object (a favorite document, folder, program, or Web page) directly from the desktop of your computer — even when you have absolutely no idea how deep the object is buried on your computer or where it may be in cyberspace. In the following list, I give you the basic lowdown on shortcuts:

✓ Shortcuts can be located anywhere on your computer, but keep them right out in the open on the desktop so that you can get right at them.

✓ When you create a shortcut for an object, Windows creates an icon for it with a name like "Shortcut to such and such." You can rename the shortcut to whatever name suits you, just as you can rename any file or folder in Windows (*see* "Naming Files and Folders" later in this part).

✔ You can always tell a shortcut icon from the regular icon because the shortcut icon contains a little box with a curved arrow pointing up to the right, like the Microsoft Word shortcut shown here.

✔ Shortcuts function just like their icon counterparts. They open the same way, and in the case of Printer shortcuts, you can drag a file to a Printer shortcut to print on the associated printer.

Shortcuts to open stuff

To create a shortcut for a folder, file, or program that resides locally on your computer and place the shortcut on the Windows XP desktop, follow these steps:

1. Select the icon of the file, folder, or application program in the My Documents or My Computer window for which you want to create a shortcut.

2. Choose File⇔Create Shortcut or right-click the icon and then choose Create Shortcut from the icon shortcut menu.

3. If Windows displays the error message "Unable to create a shortcut here. Do you want the shortcut placed on the desktop?", choose Yes. If Windows doesn't give you this error message, it places the new shortcut in the currently open window. If you want the shortcut on the desktop, where you have constant access to it, drag the shortcut icon to any place on the desktop, and release the mouse button.

If you move the file, folder, or program icon after making a shortcut to it, Windows gets all confused and displays a Missing Shortcut message dialog box. It then attempts to find out where in the blazes you moved the now-hidden component. If Windows successfully locates the component on your computer, it repairs the shortcut link and opens the component. If it can't locate the moved component (and you know where it is), use the Browse button in the Missing Shortcut dialog box to open the missing component. After you do this, Windows repairs the shortcut path so that the Missing Shortcut dialog box doesn't bother you the next time you select the shortcut icon.

You can instantly create a shortcut for any file, folder, or program icon by right-clicking the icon and then selecting Send To⇔Desktop (Create Shortcut) on the item shortcut menu. As soon as you select this command, Windows creates a shortcut icon for the selected item and places it on the Windows desktop no matter where you happen to be at the time!

If you're dealing with a really important shortcut on your desktop that you find yourself selecting all the darn time, you may want to assign a keystroke shortcut to it as well. To do this, right-click the shortcut icon on the desktop and then select Properties on the shortcut menu. Windows opens a Properties dialog box displaying the Shortcut tab with the settings for that particular shortcut.

Select the Shortcut Key text box (by clicking the cursor in it) and then type a single keyboard character (number, letter, or punctuation symbol) that you want to assign to the shortcut (this character replaces the default setting of none). This character then appears in the Shortcut key text box preceded by Ctrl+Alt+ (so that if you type the letter **g**, you see Ctrl+Alt+G). Click the OK button to close the Shortcut Properties dialog box. After that, you can launch the program opened by the shortcut simply by pressing (and holding down) the Ctrl plus Alt keys until you type the assigned character.

Shortcuts to Web pages

In addition to creating shortcuts to favorite files or folders on your computer, you can create shortcuts to favorite Web pages on the Internet. To create a shortcut to a Web page, follow these two simple steps:

1. Open the Web page for which you want to make the shortcut in Internet Explorer 6 (*see* "Browsing Web Pages" in Part II for details).

2. Choose File⇨Send⇨Shortcut To Desktop on the Internet Explorer 6 pull-down menus.

Internet shortcuts are indicated by the Web page icon (the *E* representing the Internet Explorer on top of a page) with the name of the shortcut below. When you double-click a Web page shortcut, Windows opens Internet Explorer, connects you to the Internet, and displays the target Web page.

Customizing the Desktop

The Windows desktop is the background against which all the action takes place. It contains the standard Recycle Bin icon, as well as all the desktop shortcuts you create (*see* "Creating Shortcuts," earlier in this part, for details).

The Desktop shortcut menu, which you open by right-clicking any open area of the desktop (above the taskbar), contains the following commands, which enable you to customize the look and feel of the Windows XP desktop:

✔ **Arrange Icons By:** Enables you to arrange the desktop icons by Name, Size, Type, or by date Modified. Select Auto Arrange to let Windows XP decide how to arrange them (*see* "Arranging and Sizing Icons in a Window" earlier in this part) and Align to Grid to make the icons line up on an invisible grid. You can also click Show Desktop Items to hide and then show all the desktop icons and Lock Web Items on Desktop to prevent you from inadvertently moving Web items that you download onto the desktop from the Internet (*see* "Appearance and Themes" in Part IV for details on downloading Web items onto the desktop).

✔ **Refresh:** Updates icons and Web items displayed on the desktop.

✔ **Paste:** Creates a shortcut to whatever document you're currently working on and pastes it onto the desktop.

✔ **Paste Shortcut:** Pastes whatever shortcut you've cut or copied to the Clipboard.

✔ **New:** Creates an empty folder, a file of a particular type (such as an Excel file or Word document), or a new shortcut.

✔ **Properties:** Opens the Display Properties dialog box, where you can change display stuff, such as the video settings and windows color combinations (*see* "Display" in Part IV for details).

Deleting Junk

Because the whole purpose of working on computers is to create junk, you need to know how to get rid of unneeded files and folders to free space on your hard drive. To delete files, folders, or shortcuts, follow these steps:

1. Open the folder that holds the files or folders to be deleted in the My Documents or My Computer window.

2. Select all the files, folders, or shortcuts to be deleted.

3. Choose File⇔Delete on the menu bar or press the Delete key. (You can also drag the selected Items to the Recycle Bin.)

4. Click the Yes button in the Confirm File Delete dialog box that asks whether you want to send the selected items to the Recycle Bin.

Windows XP puts all items that you delete in the Recycle Bin. The Recycle Bin is the trash can for Windows XP. Anything you delete anywhere in Windows goes into the Recycle Bin and stays there until you either retrieve the deleted item or empty the Recycle Bin.

Note that the Recycle Bin icon is a permanent item on the Windows desktop. To open this window, you simply double-click the icon on the desktop.

Use the following tips to work efficiently with the Recycle Bin:

✔ **To fill the Recycle Bin:** Select the folders or files you no longer need, drag their icons to the Recycle Bin icon on the desktop, and drop them in.

✔ **To rescue stuff from the Recycle Bin:** Open the Recycle Bin and then select the icons for the items you want to restore before you click the <u>Restore This Item</u> hyperlink (if only one item is selected) or the <u>Restore the Selected Items</u> hyperlink (if multiple items are selected). These hyperlinks are found in the navigation pane that appears on the left side of the window. Note that you can also select File⇨Restore on the pull-down menu to remove the selected item or items. You can also drag the icons for the files and folders you want to save out of the Recycle Bin and drop them in the desired location.

✔ **To rescue all the stuff in the Recycle Bin:** Open the Recycle Bin and click the <u>Restore All Items</u> hyperlink in the navigation pane of the Recycle Bin window. Note that this link is replaced by the <u>Restore This Item</u> or <u>Restore the Selected Items</u> hyperlink when you select one or more items.

✔ **To empty the Recycle Bin:** Open the Recycle Bin and click the <u>Empty Recycle Bin</u> hyperlink in the navigation pane of the Recycle Bin window, or choose File⇨Empty Recycle Bin from the menu bar. You can also empty it by right-clicking the Recycle Bin icon and choosing Empty Recycle Bin from the icon shortcut menu.

 Keep in mind that choosing the Empty Recycle Bin command immediately gets rid of everything in the Recycle Bin dialog box. Don't ever empty the Recycle Bin until after you examine the contents and are absolutely sure that you'll never need to use any of those items ever again. Delete items in the Recycle Bin only when you're sure that you're never going to need them again (or you've backed up the files on disks or some other media, such as tapes or CD-ROMs).

 If you hold down the Shift key when you press the Delete key, Windows displays a Confirm File Delete dialog box that asks whether you want to delete the selected file or files, rather than whether you want to send the files to the Recycle Bin. Click the Yes button or press Enter to delete the selected items.

Formatting a Disk

In this day and age, when floppy disk drives are rarely included in new computer systems, most of you will never experience the "joy" of formatting a floppy disk. For the rest of you who do have floppy drives on your computers and occasionally find a need to back up or transmit files on floppy disks, this section will come in handy.

Most all of the disks you purchase today are preformatted (this is done as part of the automated process that checks the disks for errors). Every once in a while, you may get a box of disks at an incredibly good price that are unformatted. You must format such disks before you can save files and folders on them.

To format a disk in drive A of your computer, follow these steps:

1. Insert a blank disk or a disk that holds files and folders that you don't give a hoot about.

2. Open the My Computer window and then right-click the icon for the Floppy Drive (A:).

3. Select the Format command from the A drive shortcut menu to open the Format 3 ½ Floppy dialog box.

4. By default, Windows XP selects high-density 3.5", 1.44MB, 512 bytes/sector as the Capacity for the size of the disk you're formatting. Choose the lesser (double-density) capacity 3.5", 720KB, 512 bytes/sector if you inserted that kind of disk into your floppy drive.

5. By default, Windows XP selects the FAT in the File System pull-down text box as the file system for which to format the disk. (This is a system supported by Windows 95, Windows for Workgroups, MS-DOS, and OS/2.) You also have a choice of selecting FAT32 as the file system (supported by Windows XP, Me, 98, and Windows 95 OEM Service Release 2) or selecting NTFS (supported by Windows XP and Windows 2000). If you select NTFS as the file system, you can also select the Enable Compression check box in the Format Options section so that you can store more data on the disk.

Don't select NTFS as the file system option if the disk is to be used on systems that also run Windows 95, 98, or Me, because these systems can't access files stored in this format.

6. (Optional) Type a label in the Volume Label text box if you want to attach a name to the disk that you can use to identify it. When you format by using the FAT system, you're restricted to 11 characters; when you're using the NTFS system, you're limited to a maximum of 32 characters.

7. (Optional) Click the Quick Format check box in the Format Options (if you're reformatting a disk that contains files and folders that you no longer need). If you're formatting a brand-new disk, leave this check box empty.

8. Click the Start button to begin formatting the disk and then click OK in the alert dialog box warning you that formatting erases all data currently on the disk.

After you click Start, Windows keeps you informed of the progress in the Formatting box at the bottom of the Format dialog box. If you need to stop the process before it's complete, click the Cancel button.

 Be sure to match the capacity setting to the physical type of disk you're using: double-density 3.5", 720KB, 512 bytes/sector or high-density 3.5", 1.44 MB, 512 bytes/sector.

 You can also format a brand-new, never-been-formatted, right-out-of-the-box disk by inserting it in the disk drive and then opening the drive icon in the My Computer window. Windows XP displays an alert box containing this message:

```
The disk in drive A is not formatted. Do you want to
format it now?
```

Click the Yes button or press Enter to open the Format dialog box, in which you can specify the disk capacity, file system, label, and so on before you start the formatting by clicking the Start button.

Getting Help and Support

Windows XP has an extensive help system that you can use not only to get general and detailed information on how to use Windows, but also to get answers from Microsoft on specific problems that you're experiencing. As in Windows 98 and Millennium Edition, Windows XP Help is an HTML document with hyperlinks that you can use to

⯈ Search for help topics by keywords.

⯈ Get help on specific topics by clicking hyperlinks such as Windows Basics and Protecting Your PC: Security Basics.

⯈ Get assisted support by connecting to the Microsoft Web site, where you can report any problems that you experience, as well as check out the status of any previously reported problems. You can even get a technician to remotely take control of your computer so that he can diagnose and troubleshoot the problem.

✔ View system information and run diagnostic utilities so that you can troubleshoot your system.

To open Windows XP Help, click the Start button on the Windows taskbar and then click Help and Support. Windows opens the Home page in the Help and Support Center window, as shown in the following figure (although your computer won't have all the Dell Online links if you have any other brand of computer). This Home page contains a number of hyperlinks, such as the What's New in Windows XP and Protecting Your PC: Security Basics links, that you can click to get quick information about particular topics.

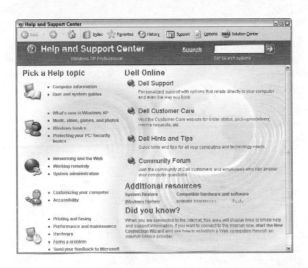

Here are some of things you can do from the Help Home page:

✔ To search for help on a particular topic, click the cursor in the Search text box at the top of the page, type your topic, and then press Enter or click the Search button. Windows returns a results page with a list of matching (or, at the very least, somewhat related topics) in the left pane. To display information on a particular topic in the frame on the right, click that hyperlink.

✔ To find a help topic in the Help index, click the Index button on the toolbar at the very top of the page. In the Type in the Keyword to Find text box, enter the first few characters of the subject you want help on to scroll to that subject in the index below. When Windows displays the topic you're interested in, click the topic to select it and then click the Display button at the bottom or double-click the topic to display the information in the frame on the right.

✓ To take a tour of Windows, click the <u>What's New in Windows XP</u> hyperlink and then click the <u>Taking a Tour or Tutorial</u> link in the Explore Windows navigation pane. Finally, click the <u>Take the Windows XP Tour</u> or <u>Take the Windows Media Player Tour</u> link that then appears in the main part of the window.

✓ To get information on your computer system, click the <u>Computer Information</u> link on the Home page and then click the <u>Detailed Computer Information</u> hyperlink in the Computer Information navigation pane.

✓ To return to a previously viewed help page, click the Back button (fl) at the top of the Help window. To then return to the page from which you came, click the Forward (–>) button.

✓ To add a help topic to the Favorites section of the Help system (so that you can return to the topic by clicking the Favorites button and then clicking a hyperlink to the topic), click the Add to Favorites button on the toolbar that appears above the help information.

✓ To print the help topic displayed in the frame on the right, click the Print button on the toolbar that appears above the help information.

Getting Info on a Disk, Folder, or File

Windows XP gives you at-a-glance information about any drive, folder, or file you select in the navigation panes of the My Computer and Windows Explorer windows. When you select a disk drive, the navigation pane shows you total capacity of the drive and the amount of free space. When you select a folder, Windows shows the name of the folder and the date and time when it was last modified. When you select a file, Windows shows the filename; file type; date and time last modified; the size (in KB); the file attribute; and, if it's a graphic file of a type that Windows can deal with, a thumbnail image.

You can also get some of this same type of information about a particular drive, folder, and file plus additional details by opening that Properties dialog box. Just open a browsing window with the drive, folder, or file that you want the lowdown on and then right-click that icon. Select the Properties command from the shortcut menu.

Disk properties

Disk properties include a wide array of statistics on the hard drive, along with tools for keeping it running at maximum. The following figure shows the Properties dialog box for my computer's hard drive.

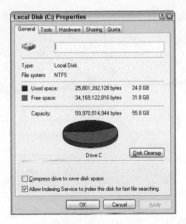

The (C:) Properties dialog box contains the following tabs and information:

✔ **General:** Shows you the name (or label) of the hard drive, the type of file system (FAT, FAT32, or NTFS), the amount of used and free space on the drive, and the drive total storage capacity (topped off with a great big pie chart just like you see in the navigation pane, only in nicer colors). This tab also includes a Disk Cleanup button that you can use to free up disk space by deleting unused files and, under the NTFS files system, a Compress Drive to Save Disk Space check box that you can check to free up disk space by compressing the files on the drive.

✔ **Tools:** Contains a Check Now button for checking the hard drive for errors, a Defragment Now button to rearrange the files on the drive in contiguous blocks (*see* "System Tools" in Part III for more on using these utilities), and a Backup Now to run the backup utility for making backup copies of your files and folders.

✔ **Hardware:** Shows you a list of the various drives on your system arranged by type (floppy, hard, and CD-ROM), with the names of the manufacturers.

✔ **Sharing:** Contains a warning that for security reasons, sharing the root drive of your computer (the C:\ drive) is not recommended, along with a link that enables you to ignore the risk and share the entire hard drive nonetheless. If you click this link, the regular Local and Network sharing and security options appear (*see* "Sharing folders on a network" earlier in this part) that you can use to set up network sharing.

✔ **Quota:** Enables you to set up disk quotas that control how many users can be sharing the drive at the same time and to allocate the maximum amount of disk space for the users. (Note that the Quota tab shows up only on drives using the NTFS file system.)

Folder properties

You can also use the Properties command to get information on individual folders on your hard drive. The Properties dialog box contains a General tab and a Customize tab. If your computer is on a network, the Properties dialog box also contains a Sharing tab — *see* "Sharing folders on a network" for details — and a Web Sharing tab.

The General tab in a folder Properties dialog box tells you the folder name; the location; size in bytes; the number of folders and files contained within the folder; last-modified date; and the folder attributes, which can be Read-Only, Archive, Hidden, and System.

The Web Sharing tab contains options for sharing the folder on a company Web site located on a corporate intranet or the World Wide Web (Internet).

Customizing a folder

The Customize tab in the Properties dialog box enables you to change the appearance of a folder. When customizing the look of a folder, you can select a picture that Windows displays on the folder when the Thumbnails view is turned on; *see* "Arranging and Sizing Icons in a Window" earlier in this part for details. You can also change the icon that Windows uses to represent the folder when you view a window in any other view besides Thumbnails (Tiles, Icons, List, and Details).

To select a ready-made folder type such as the type used for your My Pictures or My Music folders (that adds a picture or music note to the regular folder icon) as the template to use for the selected folder, click its name in the Use This Folder Type as Template drop-down list box. To apply this template to all subfolders found within the selected folder, click the Also Apply This Template to All Subfolders check box as well.

To select a new picture for Thumbnails view, click the Choose Picture button and then select the image file to use in the Browse dialog box. Remember that you can select a picture in the My Pictures folder by clicking the My Documents button on the left and then double-clicking My Pictures that then appears in the main list box.

To select a new icon for all the other views, click the Change Icon button and then click the desired icon in the Select an Icon from the List Below list box before you click OK.

To remove all the custom changes you make to a folder and restore it to its original look, select the Restore Default button.

File properties

The Properties dialog box for a file contains a General tab, a Custom tab, and a Summary tab.

The General tab in the file Properties dialog box tells you the Windows XP filename; file type; file location; size in bytes; creation date; last-edited (modified) date; last-opened (accessed) date; and the file attributes, which can be Read-Only, Archive, Hidden, and System. Please don't fool with the attributes unless you're certain that you know what you're doing.

This tab also contains a Change button to the immediate right of the Opens With option that shows the name of the program that opens the file should you double-click its file icon. To select a new program to open the file, select the Change button and then select the name of the new program in the Open With dialog box before selecting OK.

The Summary tab contains a list of fields for various attributes, such as the Title, Subject, Author, Category, Keywords, and Comments that you can fill out. The information that you fill in on the Summary tab, you can later use in searching for the file; *see* "Searching for Files and Folders" later in this part for details.

To fill in an attribute on the Summary tab, click the attribute text box and then fill in the appropriate information for use in searching for the file.

Click the Advanced button to display the summary information in an outline view. When you put the Summary tab in advanced view, you can view the attributes, but you can't modify them. To make changes, you have to click the Simple button and then click the text box of each attribute you want to change.

Launching Programs

In Windows XP, you can open the programs that you've installed on your hard drive in any one of the following three ways:

- ✔ **Select the program on the Programs menu, which you open from the Start menu:** *See* "Using the Windows Taskbar" later in this part for information about starting programs from the Start menu and manually adding items to or removing them from the Programs menu.

- ✔ **Open a shortcut to the program or to a document you open regularly:** *See* "Creating Shortcuts" earlier in this part for information about creating shortcuts for opening a program or a file that in turn opens the associated program.

- ✔ **Open a file created with the program:** *See* "Creating New Files and Folders" earlier in this part for information about opening a program by opening the file.

You can also launch programs by adding buttons for them to the Quick Launch toolbar on the taskbar and then clicking those buttons. *See* "The Quick Launch toolbar" later in this part for details.

Moving and Resizing Windows

Any window, be it a system window such as My Documents, My Computer, or the Control Panel, or a program window, such as opened by the Movie Maker or WordPad application, contains various combinations of controls and features. You can use these to modify the window and, in the case of program windows, navigate the application program.

The following list describes the features and controls found on all your typical windows:

- ✔ **Title bar:** Identifies the program or file in the opened window; also houses the Control menu, which appears when you click the program icon on the left side of the title bar.

- ✔ **Menu bar:** Contains the pull-down menus with commands specific to a program; *see* "The menu bar" later in this part.

- ✔ **Minimize button:** Shrinks the window down to a button on the taskbar.

- ✔ **Maximize button:** Zooms the window up to full size; to restore a maximized window to its former size, click the Restore Down button that replaces the Maximize button.

✔ **Close button:** Closes the window and exits any program running in it.

✔ **Toolbars:** If the window is equipped with other toolbars (such as a Standard Buttons bar), these extra toolbars are usually located below the menu bar.

✔ **Vertical scroll bar:** Enables you to vertically scroll new parts of the window into view with the up and down arrows or by dragging the scroll button.

✔ **Horizontal scroll bar:** Enables you to horizontally scroll new parts of the window into view with the right and left arrows or by dragging the scroll button.

✔ **Status bar:** Gives you different sorts of information about the current state of the program.

Here are some basic tips on dealing with the windows you encounter in Windows XP:

✔ A window must be active before you can select any of the commands or use any of the features. To activate a window, click anywhere on it. The active window is immediately placed on top of the desktop, and the title bar becomes highlighted.

✔ You can change the size of a window by dragging the borders with the mouse or by using the Size command.

✔ To move a window on the desktop, position the mouse pointer somewhere on the window title bar, and drag the outline to the new location with the mouse.

✔ If the window contains a toolbar, and you don't have a clue as to what the tool does, point to the tool button, and Windows displays a ScreenTip with the tool name.

You can move windows around the desktop and resize them from full-screen (called *maximized*) all the way down to wee buttons on the taskbar (called *minimized*) at your convenience.

To move a window, follow these steps:

1. If necessary, restore the window to an in-between size, either by clicking the Restore Down button, if the window is maximized, or by clicking the taskbar button, if the window is minimized.

2. Position the mouse pointer over the window title bar.

3. Drag the outline of the window to the new location on the desktop.

4. Release the mouse button to drop the window in the new location on the desktop.

To maximize a window, you have two methods to choose between:

✓ Click the Maximize button on the window title bar if the window is displayed at less than full size. (The Maximize button is located in the middle of the three buttons on the right side of the title bar.) Otherwise, click the window taskbar button if the window is minimized.

✓ Choose Maximize from the window Control menu (which you open by clicking the program icon in the far-left side of the window title bar).

Remember that after you maximize a window, you can restore the window to the original size by doing one of these two things:

✓ Click the Restore Down button on the window title bar. (The Restore button is located in the middle of the three buttons on the right side of the title bar.)

✓ Choose Restore from the window Control menu (which you open by clicking the program icon in the far-left side of the window title bar).

To minimize a window to just a button on the taskbar, you can do either of the following:

✓ Click the Minimize button on the window title bar. (The Minimize button is the one with the minus sign, located on the left of the three buttons on the right side of the title bar.)

✓ Choose Minimize from the window Control menu (which you open by clicking the program icon in the far-left side of the window title bar).

In addition to using the automatic sizing controls, you can manually size a window (assuming that it's not currently minimized or maximized) by dragging any of the sides or corners. You can always tell when Windows XP will allow you to move one or more of the sides of a window by dragging, because the mouse pointer changes from the standard pointer to a double-headed arrow.

Keep the following points in mind to get the most out of resizing windows while you work:

✓ Move a window whenever something else (such as the taskbar or another window) gets in the way so that you can't see the window contents.

✓ Maximize a window when you're doing some serious work (or playing) in that window and don't need the distraction of all the other junk that populates the Windows XP desktop.

✔ Minimize a window when you still need it open (especially when it's running processes, such as printing or calculating, in the background) but won't be directly using those features for a while.

✔ Keep the window sized in-between when you need to see part of those contents on the desktop at the same time as you're doing something else (as when moving or copying with drag-and-drop).

See "Control menus" later in this part for information on how to use the Control menu to size and move windows.

Naming Files and Folders

Files contain all the precious data that you create with those sophisticated (and expensive) Windows-based programs. Files occupy a certain amount of space rated either in kilobytes (KB), or thousands of bytes) or megabytes (MB, or millions of bytes) on a particular disk, be it your hard drive, a CD-ROM, DVD disc, or even a removable floppy disk.

The location of a file (the *pathname*) is identified by the letter of the drive that holds the disk, the folder or subfolders within which it's embedded, and a unique filename. A typical pathname could look like this:

```
C:\Accounts\Payables\invoice 0215.xls
```

This pathname is shorthand to indicate that a file named "invoice 0215.xls" is located in a folder named "Payables," which is itself located in a folder called "Accounts," which is, in turn, located on drive C (the hard drive) of your computer.

Folders are the data containers in Windows XP. They can contain files or other folders, or a combination of files and folders. Like files, folders occupy a certain amount of space (rated in KB or MB) on the particular drive.

The location of a folder (known in techese as the folder *directory path*) is identified by the letter of the drive that holds the disk, the other folder or folders within which it's embedded, and a unique name. The following is an example of a Workstuff folder directory path, which indicates that Workstuff is a subfolder within the My Documents folder on drive C:

```
C:\My Documents\Workstuff
```

You can locate folders in the My Documents, Windows Explorer, and My Computer windows; **see** "Browsing Drives, Folders, and Files on the Computer" earlier in this part. To find out more about the ins and outs of folders in Windows XP, *see also* "Creating New Files and Folders," "Copying (and Moving) Files and Folders," and "Deleting Junk," all earlier in this part.

Long filenames

Each filename in Windows consists of two parts: a main filename and a file extension. The file extension, which identifies the type of file and what program created it, consists of a maximum of three characters that are automatically assigned by the creating agent or program. Typically, these file extensions aren't displayed in the lists of filenames that you see. For information on how to display the file extensions, *see* "Opening Files and Folders" later in this part.

Whereas the creating program normally assigns the file extension, Windows XP enables you to call the main part of the filename whatever the heck you want, up to a maximum of 255 characters (including spaces!). Keep in mind, however, that all pre-Windows 95 programs, and even some that run on Windows 98, don't support long filenames. These programs allow a maximum of only eight characters, with no spaces.

File icons

In Windows XP, files are assigned special icons along with the filenames. These icons help you quickly identify the type of file when you're browsing the files in your folders in My Documents, My Computer, or Internet Explorer 6. The following table shows some examples of these icons:

File Icon	*File Type and Program That Opens It*
China2003.MSWMM	Movie Maker program file that runs the Movie Maker program on your computer
Bibliography.doc	Word document that will open in Word for Windows
Excel TST.xls	Excel workbook that will open in Excel for Windows
DirectX.log	Text file that will open in Notepad utility
Home Page.htm	HTML document that will open in Internet Explorer 6
ORIGINAL.SET	Unidentified generic file that will open the Open With dialog box, which asks you to identify a program that can open the file

Things you do with files

A few things you will inevitably do with files (in no particular order) are the following:

🖊 Open a file (and, if necessary, the program that created it, if that program is identifiable) by double-clicking or highlighting and then clicking the file icon, depending on the Folder Options settings you specify. *See* "Opening Files and Folders" later in this part for details on customizing the click settings.

🖊 Print files (via the associated program) by dragging the file icons to a printer in the Printer folders or to a printer shortcut on the desktop.

🖊 Move or copy files by dragging the file icons to new folders. *See* "Copying (and Moving) Files and Folders" earlier in this part for details.

🖊 Get rid of files (and free the space they're taking up) when they're no longer of any use to you by selecting those icons and pressing the Delete key or by dragging the icons to the Recycle Bin; *see* "Deleting Junk" earlier in this part for details.

As in earlier versions of Windows, you can create shortcuts to file locations in Windows XP to quickly access frequently used files, folders, or Web pages; *see* "Creating Shortcuts" earlier in this part for details.

Also, keep in mind that you can get lots of good information on a file — such as which program created it, how big it is, when it was created and last revised, and so on — by choosing the Properties command on the file shortcut menu. For details, *see* "Getting Info on a Disk, Folder, or File" earlier in this part.

Renaming files and folders

You can rename file and folder icons directly in Windows XP by typing over or editing the existing file or folder name, as I outline in these steps:

1. Open the My Documents, Windows Explorer, or My Computer window that contains the folder or file you want to rename.

2. Right-click the file or folder icon, and select Rename on the shortcut menu.

3. Type the new name that you want to give the folder (up to 255 characters) or edit the existing name. You can use the Delete key to remove characters and the → or ← key to move the cursor without deleting characters.

4. When you finish editing the file or folder name, press the Enter key to complete the renaming procedure.

When the file or folder name is selected for editing, typing anything entirely replaces the current name. If you want to edit the file or folder name rather than replace it, you need to click the insertion point at the place in the name that needs editing before you begin typing.

Opening Files and Folders

The most common way to open a file or folder is to open that icon in the Windows Explorer, My Documents, or My Computer windows. *See* "Browsing Drives, Folders, and Files on the Computer" earlier in this part for details.

How you open the file or folder icon after you have it displayed in a browsing window depends on the Folder Options settings that your computer uses:

✔ Single-click the icon when you've selected the Single-Click to Open an Item (Point to Select) option in the Folder Options dialog box for single-clicking to open and mousing over to select.

✔ Double-click the icon when you use the Double-Click to Open an Item (Single-Click to Select) option in the Folder Options dialog box for double-clicking to open and single-clicking for selecting. Note that this is the default way of doing things in Windows unless you've changed this setting in the Folder Options dialog box (Tools➪Folder Options).

Remember that you can also open a file or folder by right-clicking that icon and then choosing the Open command at the top of the shortcut menu.

Traditionally, *graphical user interfaces* (known affectionately as GUIs), such as Windows, use the following mouse-click scheme to differentiate between selecting and opening the icon:

✔ Single-click the icon to select it (indicated on-screen by high-lighting the icon and the filename or folder name).

✔ Double-click the icon to open that object. *See* "File icons" in the preceding section for details on the different types of Windows objects.

Hyperlinks, made popular on Web pages on the World Wide Web, however, use a slightly different mouse-click scheme to differentiate between selecting and following (the equivalent of opening) the links, which can be attached to graphics or text on the page:

✔ Move the mouse pointer over the hyperlink to select it (indicated by the mouse pointer's changing to the hand icon).

✔ Click (don't double-click) the hyperlink to follow the link. (Normally, following the link means to jump to another section of the page or to open a completely different Web page.)

In Windows XP, you can choose between selecting and opening Windows icons the normal GUI way (single- and double-click) or the normal Web way (point at and click).

When Windows XP is first installed on your computer, the traditional GUI single- and double-click scheme is in effect. If you want to switch over and experiment with the Web point-and-click system, you can do so at any time by making the following modifications to the Folders Options:

1. Click the Start button on the taskbar and then click My Computer to open the My Computer window (you can also do this from the My Documents window).

2. Choose Tools⇨Folder Options on the window menu bar to open the Folder Options dialog box.

3. Click the Single-Click to Open an Item (Point to Select) radio button near the bottom of the General tab in this dialog box.

4. (Optional) By default, Windows underlines icon titles at all times. If you want the titles underlined only when you mouse over them, click the Underline Icon Titles Only When I Point at Them radio button.

5. Click the OK button to close the Folder Options dialog box and put your new single-click settings in effect.

See also "Selecting Files and Folders" later in this part for information about selecting files and folders after the folder is open.

Playing Music, Video, and Movies

Windows XP includes Windows Media Player for playing music and videos on your computer. You use Windows Media Player to play audio or video CD-ROMs saved on your computer (or, if you have a fast enough connection, audio or video as it is being downloaded to your computer from a site on the World Wide Web), MP3 music files, or even DVD discs (the newest format for feature-length movies that can include not only the film, but also special interactive clips, such as outtakes and trailers) if your computer is equipped with a special DVD drive.

Windows Media Player

You can use Windows Media Player to play audio, video, and animation files that you either save on your computer or (if you have a fast connection to the Internet, also known as *broadband*) play online as they're being downloaded to your computer (a technique known as *streaming*). This means that you can use Windows Media Player to play Internet radio stations, as well as to view video clips from trailers from upcoming movies. Of course, the most important thing is that Windows Media Player also plays all the MP3 (short for MPEG3, which is a compression scheme developed by the Motion Picture Entertainment industry) audio files that you've bootlegged — I mean, downloaded — from your favorite music Web sites.

You're able to view Windows Media Player in one of two modes: full mode (Ctrl+1) and compact or skin mode (Ctrl+2). Full mode (shown in the following figure) is the default.

When you use Windows Media Player in full mode, it displays a taskbar on the left side of the player that contains a number of buttons that you can use to switch between the types of media that you're playing and to control how you view and play them:

- **Now Playing:** When playing audio, this pane represents the pattern of sounds being played visually as waves of particles. When playing a video file, the video appears centered in the Windows Media Player screen.

- **Media Guide (selected by default):** Enables you to find music and videos to play with Windows Media Player. When this button is selected, Windows attempts to connect you to the WindowsMedia.com Web site, where you can locate and download all sorts of audio and video files.

- **Copy from CD:** Enables you to display the tracks of the audio CD that you've placed into your computer CD-ROM drive. To play a particular track on the CD, double-click the description in the track list. To copy the tracks from the CD onto your hard drive, click the Copy Music button at the top of the Media Player.

✔ **Media Library:** Enables you to display an outline with all the audio and video media files on your hard drive. If you copied tracks from audio CDs (by using the Copy Music button in the Copy from view), you can play these tracks by double-clicking them in the Media Library list. If you've created presets to various online radio stations, you can connect to the stations by double-clicking the presets in this view.

✔ **Radio Tuner:** Enables you to play any of the preset online radio stations, to search for new radio stations, or to create or edit the lists of preset stations.

✔ **Copy to CD or Device:** Enables you to copy the music you're playing to a recordable CD-ROM drive or a particular portable device (such as a pocket PC, smart cell phone, or a portable MP3 player) that's connected to your computer.

✔ **Premium Services:** Contains links to various subscription services (this means they cost you money) that enable you to download and stream both audio and video digital media.

✔ **Skin Chooser:** Enables you to select a new appearance (skin) for Windows Media Player when it's in compact or skin mode (Ctrl+2). In this pane, you can select any of the included skins for compact mode, or you can download new skins from the Web.

To hide the display of the Windows Media Player taskbar, click the Hide Taskbar button (the very thin button with > that appears to the immediate right of the Copy to CD or Device taskbar button). When you click this button, it immediately turns into a Show Taskbar button (indicated by the < on the button) that you can click to redisplay the Windows Media Player taskbar.

To listen to your tunes without having Windows Media Player obscure any part of the computer screen, play Windows Media Player in mini-mode. To do this, right-click the Windows taskbar and then click Toolbars⇨Windows Media Player on the shortcut menu. After that, when you click the Minimize button in the upper-right corner of the player window, Windows reduces the player to a button on the Windows taskbar, complete with playback controls. In mini-mode, you can display the audio visualization usually shown in the Now Playing pane by clicking the Show Video and Visualization Window button at the far-right side of the minimized Windows Media Player. To open a menu with options for selecting new music from among your downloaded albums, playlists, radio stations, and the like, click the Quick Access Panel button to the immediate left of the Windows Media Player icon at the far-left side of the minimized player. To display the name of the album and track currently playing, position the mouse pointer over this Windows Media Player icon. To restore the player to its previous size, click the Restore button, located immediately below the Show Video and Visualization Window button.

Audio CD-ROMs

With a CD-ROM or DVD drive, a sound card, and some cool speakers, you can listen to music while you work. Today's CD-ROM drives can play audio CDs (compact discs), as well as CD-ROMs with multimedia programs, such as encyclopedias and games, games, games; *see* "Multimedia CD-ROMs" later in this part for details.

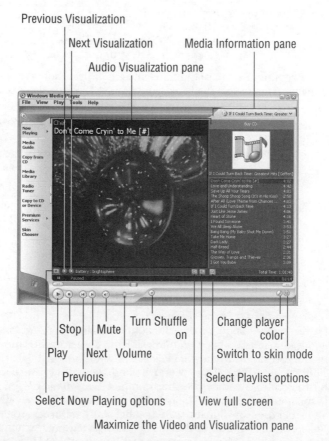

Previous Visualization

Next Visualization   Media Information pane

Audio Visualization pane

Stop   Mute   Turn Shuffle   Change player
                        on   color

Play   Next   Volume   Switch to skin mode

Previous   Select Playlist options

Select Now Playing options   View full screen

Maximize the Video and Visualization pane

To play a favorite audio compact disc in your CD-ROM player with Windows Media Player, follow these steps:

1. Insert the CD (the shiny side with rainbows and no writing) face down in the CD-ROM drive.

2. When you close the door on the CD-ROM drive, Windows reads information that tells it that the CD is of the audio (compact disc) type rather than the data (CD-ROM) type, and then Windows automatically opens the Audio CD window, where you can click Play Audio CD Using Windows Media Player (if it's not automatically selected) and then click the OK button.

If the Audio CD window doesn't automatically open when you pop an audio CD into your CD-ROM drive, click the Start button and then click All Programs⇨Accessories⇨Entertainment⇨Windows Media Player to jump-start the window. If you have an Internet connection, and the album information doesn't automatically appear in the Media Information pane on the right side of the Windows Media Player window, you can possibly get a list of tracks on the album by clicking the Find Album Info link in the Unknown Album designation at the top of this pane.

After the CD starts playing in Now Playing mode in the Media Player, you can pause it by clicking the pause button (the one with two vertical bars). To restart the CD, click the play button (the one with the triangle pointing to the right that replaces the Pause button). If you want to stop the CD, click the Stop button (the one with the square).

Note that you can control the volume for the CD Player by dragging the vertical volume control (appearing in the triangle that looks like a ramp to the right of the Stop button). Drag this control to the right (to increase the volume) or to the left (to decrease the volume). To temporarily mute the player, click the mute button (the tiny button with the picture of the speaker to the immediate left of the volume control). To turn off the mute, just click the mute button a second time.

When playing the disc in the Copy to CD mode, you can do any of the following things to enhance your listening enjoyment:

✔ To replace the audio visualization with liner-note-type album information, select View⇨Info Center View, followed by the Always Show and Show Only When Detailed Media Information Is Available items. Windows then replaces the visualization with the Info Center view that shows the album details. You can also display artist information, lyrics (available only when you copy the tracks to your computer's hard disk), related music, and tag information (that gives you lowdown on the currently playing track, (including the composer and band or orchestra, when available).

🖛 To copy the disc that's playing onto your hard drive (starting
with the track that's currently playing), click the Copy from CD
button. Remove the check mark from any track that you don't
want copied to CD (by clicking its check box, since all tracks
are automatically selected when you first click open this pane),
insert a blank CD disc into your computer's CD or DVD drive
and then click the Copy Music button at the top of the Copy
from CD pane.

When playing the audio disc in the Now Playing mode, you can do
any of the following things to enhance your listening enjoyment:

🖛 To select the next variation of the current type of visual representation of the music shown in the Windows Media Player
window, click the Next Visualization button. To return to a previous representation, click the Previous Visualization button.

🖛 To maximize the visualization (or video, when playing a video
clip or DVD disc) in the Now Playing pane by hiding the Media
Information pane on the right side that shows the album cover
and track list (if this information is available from an online
database of album information), click the Maximize the Video
and Visualization Pane button.

🖛 To view the audio visualization (or video clip or DVD) full-screen,
click the View Full Screen button. To return the screen to normal
after making the audio visualization full-screen, click the mouse
anywhere on-screen.

🖛 To select a new visualization of a different category, click the
Select Now Playing Options button and then select the
Visualizations submenu, followed by the name of the type and
the name of the visualization on their submenus.

🖛 To display the SRS Wow Effects, which add bass and generally
enhance the depth of your speakers, select View⇨Enhance-
ments⇨SRS WOW Effects on the Media Player menu bar. To
turn on the effect, click the Turn Off link. If your computer has
large separate speakers, click the Normal Speaker link until it
reads Large Speakers. If you're listening to the music with
headphones, click the Large Speakers link once to change it to
Headphones. To adjust the base, drag the TruBass slider to the
left or right. To enhance the stereo effect, drag the WOW Effect
slider until the sound is optimized.

🖛 To display a graphic equalizer in a pane at the bottom of
Windows Media Player that enables you to tweak the sound,
select View⇨Enhancements⇨Graphic Equalizer on the Media
Player menu bar. To select a new preset, click the drop-down
button attached to the Default link and then click the preset
you want on the pop-up menu. To customize one of the presets

even further, drag the various sliders up and down until you're happy with the sound. By default, the sliders are set to move together in a loose group. To move them in a tight group, click the Set Equalizer Sliders to Move in a Tight Group option button (the one right below the Set Equalizer Sliders to Move Together in a Loose Group option button, which is automatically selected). To move the sliders independently, click the Set Equalizer Sliders to Move Independently option button (the one at top of the group of three to the left to the sliders themselves).

✔ To go online to download plug-ins that enhance the capabilities of Windows Media Player, select View⇨Plug-Ins⇨Download Plug-Ins on the menu bar. Windows then opens the Windows Media 9 Series download page, where you can download plug-ins such as those that enhance the quality of the audio and video playback in Windows Media Player and enable you to copy music to your computer in the ever-popular MP3 audio format.

✔ To shuffle the order in which the tracks are played, click the Turn Shuffle On button at the bottom of the Windows Media Player window. Windows Media Player then plays the album tracks in a random order. To return to the album's original order again, click the Shuffle button a second time.

Radio stations

If you have a connection to the Internet, you can use the radio tuner in Windows Media Player to play your favorite Internet radio stations. To play an Internet radio station, open Windows Media Player by clicking the Start button and then clicking Windows Media Player on the left side of the Start menu. In the Media Player, click the Radio Tuner button in the panel on the left.

When you click the Radio Tuner button, Windows Media Player displays a list of featured stations above the My Stations and Recently Played Stations bands at the bottom of this list. and the links to the Find More Stations categories and Search Keyword text box to the right:

✔ To add a featured station in the list to your My Stations, click the name of the station to expand it and then click its Add to My Stations link. Click the station name a second time to reduce the station info to a single row.

✔ To play a station in the Featured Stations list, click its station name in the list to expand it and then click the Play link (for some stations, this link appears as Visit Website to Play). Windows then connects you to the station's Web page and, after connecting to it, begins playing its current broadcast.

✔ To find more Internet radio stations, click the link for the category you're interested in (Top 40, Country, New Age, and so on); then click the name of the station to expand it and either click its <u>Add to My Stations</u> link to add it to your favorites or click its <u>Play</u> or <u>Visit Website to Play</u> link. To return to the initial screen, click the Back button. To return to your My Stations pane, click the <u>Return to My Stations</u> link.

✔ To open the My Stations pane that contains links to all the radio stations you added as favorites, click the My Stations button at the far-right side of the My Stations band. Windows then opens a new pane that contains a list of all the stations you added. To play the station, click its name and then click its Play or Visit Website to Play link. To remove the station from My Favorites, click the Remove from My Stations link.

✔ To open the Recently Played Stations pane, which contains links to all the radio stations you've listened to of late, click the Recently Played Stations button at the far-right side of the Recently Played Stations band. Windows then opens a new pane that contains a list of all the stations you added. To play the station, click its name and then click its <u>Play</u> or <u>Visit Website to Play</u> link. To add the station to My Favorites, click the <u>Add to My Stations</u> link.

✔ To search for a particular Internet radio station, click the Search Keyword text box on the right side of the Station Finder pane and then replace the text Search Keyword with your own search text before you click the Click to Search button (the green one with the white arrow to the immediate right of this text box).

Copying audio files and making CDs

If your hard drive has sufficient room, you can copy music that you play with the CD Player. When you copy tracks from an audio CD, Windows automatically compresses them (otherwise, you'd end up sacrificing hundreds of megabytes of storage space to the likes of Nora Jones). After copying tracks from an audio CD, you can then add those songs to your own playlists, and if your computer has a CDR drive (a CD-ROM that is capable of not only playing, but also recording CDs), you can then burn your own audio CDs.

Copying music to your hard drive

To copy tracks from an Audio CD, click the Copy from CD button in Windows Media Player. The player automatically marks all tracks for copying by putting check marks in each of the check boxes preceding the number and title of the CD tracks. To copy the entire CD-ROM, go ahead and click the Copy Music button at the top of the Windows Media Player window. To skip some of the tracks, click the check boxes of the tracks you don't want copied to remove those check marks before you click the Copy from CD button.

When you click the Copy Music button, Windows opens a Copy Options (1 of 2) dialog box, containing the following options:

- **Add Copy Protection to Your Music:** Select this radio button to limit the playing of the copied tracks to your computer and secured devices such as your portable MP3 player.

- **Do Not Add Copy Protection to Your Music:** Select this radio button to be able to play the copied tracks on your computer or any other computer or connected device that you later care to copy them to.

- **I Understand that Music Copied from CD's Is Protected by Law...:** You must select this long-winded check box (implicating you in the upholding of international copyright law as it pertains to music piracy) after selecting either the Add Copy Protection to Your Music or the Do Not Add Copy Protection to Your Music radio button in order to active the Next> button.

When you select the Next> button after choosing between adding and not adding copy-protection radio buttons and selecting the "I Understand" check box, Windows displays the Copy Options (2 of 2) dialog box, which contains these additional two radio buttons to choose between:

- **Change My Current Format Settings:** Pick this option to change the audio format used in copying the selected tracks and/or the audio quality in the Options dialog box. Windows Media Player 9 supports two new audio formats, Windows Media Audio (variable rate) and Windows Media Lossless, in addition to the normal Windows Media Audio format. Both of these new audio formats create smaller file sizes than the normal Windows Media Audio format and claim to create better quality than the MP3 audio format.

- **Keep My Current Format Settings:** Select this option to retain your current audio-format and audio-quality settings.

After selecting either the Change My Current Format Settings (and selecting the new audio-format and/or audio-quality settings in the Options dialog box) or the Keep My Current Format Settings radio button, you need to select the Finish button to have Windows begin copying the marked tracks.

The Copy Status column in Windows Media Player keeps you informed of the progress in copying each of the marked tracks. To stop the copying of a track, click the Stop Copy button (which replaces the Copy Music button). To listen to the CD as the tracks are copied onto your hard drive, click the Play button after you click the Copy Music button.

To change the compression level that Windows Media Player uses when recording audio files on your hard drive, click Tools⇨Options and then click the Devices tab. This tab lists all of the devices, such as CD drives, and portable devices, such as handheld computers or portable MP3 players, that you've connected to your system. Double-click the name of the device for which you want to change the compression, click the Data CD tab, and then click the Select Quality Level radio button and drag the slider beneath it to the left (to decrease the quality by increasing the compression) or right (to increase the quality and decrease the amount of compression). Click OK twice to close the Properties dialog box and the Options dialog box.

Creating playlists

After copying audio CD tracks, you can organize them into playlists that determine the group the songs are in and control the order in which they're played. To create a new playlist for your songs, follow these steps:

1. Click the Media Library button in Windows Media Player.

2. Click the Playlist button at the top of the Media Player window and then click New Playlist on the pop-up menu.

Note that the first time you select the Playlist button, Windows searches your computer system for all types of media files (both audio and video).

3. Enter a name for the playlist in the Playlist Name text box provided by the New Playlist dialog box.

4. Click the appropriate icon the View Media Library pane on the left of the New Playlist dialog box to display its tracks. Select Album in the View Media Library by drop-down list box to view the contents of the Media Library by album. Select Artist instead if you want the contents of the Media Library listed by artist.

5. Add the songs you want in the new playlist by clicking their tracks: to select a continuous list of songs. Click the first one and then hold down Shift as you click the last one. To select individual songs that aren't next to one another, hold down Ctrl as you click each one.

6. To change the order in which the tracks you add to the playlist are played, click a track name and then click either the Promote button (the one with the blue arrow pointing up) or the Demote button (the one with the blue arrow pointing down) until the track appears at the desired place in the playlist.

7. When you finish adding tracks to your new playlist, click the OK button to close the New Playlist dialog box.

To verify that your new playlist contains all the tracks you intended to add, scroll down the media file outline in the left pane of the Windows Media Player window until you see the name of your playlist under the heading My Playlists and then click that icon to display the contents in the pane on the right. To play a song in a playlist, select that playlist in the My Playlists section of the media files outline in the left pane of the Windows Media Player window and then double-click the song title in the pane on the right.

To add or delete tracks from a playlist, click its name in the View Media Library pane on the left and then click the Playlists button, followed by the Edit Playlist item on the pop-up menu. To add a new track to the list, simply locate and click its name in the View Media Library pane of the Edit Playlist dialog box. To delete a track, right-click its name in the playlist pane on the right and then click Delete from Playlist on its shortcut menu.

Recording audio CDs

If your computer is equipped with a CD-R or CD-RW drive, you can make your own audio CDs. A CD-R drive is a CD recordable drive that is capable of making only one copy to a blank CD. A CD-RW drive or a CD rewritable drive is capable of copying tracks on the same CD multiple times. CDs recorded with a CD-R drive can be played on any CD player (including portable CD players, such as the Sony Discman). CDs recorded with a CD-RW drive, however, can only be played on CD-ROM drives like the one connected to your computer.

Before you can record audio files to a blank CD, you must organize the tracks into a playlist (*see* the previous section, "Creating playlists," for details). The Adaptec CD Recording plug-in that does the recording in Windows Media Player can record audio files saved in any of the following audio formats:

✔ MP3 audio files (which use the .MP3 file extension)

✔ Windows audio files (which use the .wav file extension)

✔ Windows Media Audio files (which use the .wma file extension and are the type of files that Windows Media Player uses when you copy music from your CDs or the Internet radio)

If you're copying a CD with a CD-R drive, be sure that the songs in your playlist use most of the space on the new CD, as you won't have a second chance to burn the CD. Also, check to make sure that songs in your playlist run no longer than 74 minutes total (or 650MB), because this is the longest amount of music that you can record on a blank CD with a CD-R.

To record the tracks in your playlists on a blank CD, put a new recordable CD in the computer CD-R or CD-RW drive and then follow these steps:

1. Open Windows Media Player by clicking the Start button and then clicking Windows Media Player on the left side of the Start menu.

2. Click the Copy Selected Items to CD button (labeled simply Copy) or select File➪Copy➪Copy to Audio CD on the Windows Media Player menu to open the Playlists dialog box.

3. Click the name of the playlist you want to add to the CD in the Items to Copy drop-down list box and then click the Copy button. During the copying process, the CD Recording plug-in transcodes each file by converting and compressing the file in a temporary location on your computer. After the files are transcoded, the copying process begins. Note that the CD isn't finished until Complete appears for each track in the list shown in the Adaptec CD Recording Plug-in dialog box. When the recording of the last track is complete, you will briefly see a Closing Disc message before the dialog box closes, and Windows automatically ejects the CD-ROM from the computer's CD or DVD drive.

If you don't have the rights to make disc copies of the tracks in your playlist, the CD Recording plug-in displays an "error has occurred" message in the Status column after the name of the track instead of the normal "copying," which changes to "converted" status during the track's transcoding (thus preventing you from copying that track to a new CD disc). The only way you obtain the rights to copy a track onto a new CD-ROM is by purchasing it in some manner. You do this most commonly by purchasing and downloading the track from an online music store or by copying it onto your hard disk from a commercially produced CD.

The compression quality that you use to copy tracks from an audio CD to the Media Library on your computer determines the sound quality of the tracks, but not the length. When you copy tracks from a playlist in your Media Library to a blank CD, the tracks of the new CD reflect the sound quality used. Provided you have sufficient space on your hard drive, you should use the highest possible sound quality when recording tracks from a CD onto your hard drive that you intend later to copy to CDs made with your computer CD-R or CD-RW drive.

To increase the sound quality before recording tracks on your hard drive, click Tools➪Options on the Windows Media Player menu and then click the Copy Music tab in the Options dialog box. Drag the Audio Quality slider to the right until you reach the quality that you have hard drive space for (the message beneath the slider keeps you informed of how many megabytes are required to burn an entire CD at each quality setting you select). Also, be sure that the Digital Copying and Use Error Correction check boxes are both selected before you close the Options dialog box.

Video files

Most of the time, Windows Media Player automatically opens in Now Playing mode whenever you open a video file that requires it to play. However, you can start Windows Media Player yourself and then browse to and open the video file you want to play. To open Windows Media Player, you click the Start button on the Windows taskbar and then click Windows Media Player on the left side of the Start menu.

To play a local video file (that is, one that's been saved on your hard drive or a CD-ROM), choose the File➪Open command (Ctrl+O) and then enter the pathname of the file in the Open text box, or use the Browse button to locate it in a standard Open dialog box.

If you keep your video clips and movies in the My Videos folder, you can open this folder by clicking the My Documents button on the left side of the Open dialog box and then double-clicking My Videos in the main list box.

After the video starts playing, you can pause it by clicking the Pause button (the one with two vertical bars). To restart the video, click the Play button (the one with the triangle pointing to the right that replaces the Pause button). If you want to stop the video, click the Stop button (the one with the square).

You can control the video volume by dragging the vertical volume control (appearing in the triangle that looks like a ramp to the right of the Stop button). Drag this control to the right (to increase the volume) or to the left (to decrease the volume). To temporarily mute the player, click the mute button (the tiny button with the picture of the speaker to the immediate left of the volume control). To turn off the mute, just click the mute button a second time.

When viewing a video in Now Playing mode, you can control the following settings:

✔ **To display the video playlist** (if it has one) in a pane on the right side of the Windows Media Player screen, select View⇨ Now Playing Options⇨Show Playlist on the Windows Media Player menu bar. To play a particular track in the video clip, double-click the description in the list.

✔ **To modify the color settings,** adjust the brightness and contrast, or change the size, choose View⇨Enhancements⇨Video Settings on the Media Player pull-down menus. To change the color settings or adjust the brightness or contrast, drag the appropriately marked slider. To reset the video to the original settings, click the link marked Reset. To change the size of the video in Windows Media Player, click the Select Video Zoom Settings link and then select the appropriate size from the pop-up menu (50%, 100%, or 200%).

DVDs

Windows Media Player can now play movies and other video content that's been recorded on DVDs (alternatively known as Digital Versatile Discs or Digital Video Discs). Like conventional DVD players, the Windows Media Player can skip to specific chapters, play sequences in slow motion, and switch the audio and caption languages. You can also use your connection to the Internet to download extra information about the title you're playing.

In order to use Windows Media Player to play DVD-based movies and other video, you must have a special DVD drive (your regular CD-ROM drive isn't going to do it) and a DVD decoder installed on your computer. Note, however, that DVD drives can read both audio CD-ROMs and DVD discs. To play a DVD with the Windows Media Player, you simply pop the disc into your drive and wait for the Media Player window to open.

If the Windows Media Player window doesn't open automatically, you can open it manually: Click the Start button and then click Windows Media Player on the left side of the Start menu.

After the Windows Media Player window opens, click the Media Library button and then select the DVD to play by clicking the My Playlist button in the media list in the left pane, followed by the name of the DVD in the pane on the right.

After selecting the DVD, you can play, pause, stop, and eject the disc as follows:

✔ **To start playing the DVD disc,** click the Play button (the one with the triangle pointing to the right) or select Play⇨Play/Pause on the menu bar (Ctrl+P).

✔ **To pause the DVD disc,** click the Pause button (the one with two vertical bars) or select Play⇨Play/Pause on the menu bar (Ctrl+P).

✔ **To stop playing the DVD disc,** click the Stop button (the one with the square) or select Play⇨Stop (Ctrl+S).

✔ **To eject the DVD disc,** select Play⇨Eject on the menu bar or press Ctrl+E.

Note that when playing a DVD with Windows Media Player, you get the best results if you turn off any screen savers and make sure that the system hibernation setting is turned off. *See* "Appearance and Themes" in Part IV for information on turning off your screen saver and "Shutting Down Windows" later in this part for details on the hibernation setting.

Many DVD discs have their own menu system, which you can use as well to play the movie; set up screen and sound options; and select special features, such as trailers and interviews with the stars. To access these menu options, position the mouse pointer (in the shape of a hand) over the menu item and then click the item. To return the main menu screen at any time when viewing the contents of the DVD disc, click the Open Menu (Top Menu) button in the lower-left corner of the screen.

To play the movie in full-screen mode, press Alt+Enter. If you want to hide the playlist while you view the video, click the Hide Playlist button in the lower-right corner of the screen. To exit full-screen mode, click the Exit Full Screen button to the immediate right of the Show Playlist button (which replaces the Hide Playlist button as soon as you click it).

If the DVD is divided into several titles, you can jump to a new section in the DVD by first displaying the playlist pane and then double-clicking the name of the title to go to in the playlist. If the titles are then divided into chapters, you can jump directly to a particular scene in the title by double-clicking its name in the playlist.

Portable device

You can use the Copy to CD or Device button in Windows Media Player to copy music to handheld devices, which include pocket PCs (such as the Compaq iPAQ and the HP Jornada), PDAs (Personal Digital Assistants, such as the Palm PalmPilot III and Casio Cassiopeia), portable MP3 players, and even some types of smart cell phones. Before you can use Windows Media Player to copy music files, you must establish a connection between the desktop computer running Windows XP and your handheld device. This connection is most often made via a cable or, in some cases, a cradle that connects the two devices with a USB or serial cable.

After you've connected a portable device to the desktop computer running Windows XP, open Windows Media Player on the desktop computer by clicking the Start button on the taskbar and then clicking the Copy to CD or Device button on the left side.

When you click this button, Windows divides the Windows Media Player window into a left pane called Music to Copy and a right pane called Music on Device. You then follow these steps to copy music files from the Media Library to your handheld device:

1. Click the Media Library button on the left side of Windows Media Player, and select the tracks you want to copy; *see* "Creating playlists" earlier in this part for details on selecting tunes.

2. Click the Copy to CD or Device button on the left side of Windows Media Player. The tracks that you selected in the Media Library are now displayed in the Music to Copy pane.

3. Select the folder on the portable device into which you want to copy the selected tracks. If your portable device has a sepa-rate storage card that acts like a second hard drive, and you want to copy the music onto this card, select it by clicking the drop-down button to the right of the name of the device, and select the card on the pop-up menu. If Windows Media Player is having trouble finding the portable device and listing the folders, press F5, or if you connect through a cradle, remove and then reseat the device in the cradle.

4. Each of the tracks you selected for copying in the Media library has a check mark in the check box that precedes the name and description. If you decide that you don't want to copy some of the tracks or don't have room to copy them, click the check boxes to remove the check marks.

5. Click the Copy Music button in the top right of Windows Media Player to copy all of the marked tracks in the Music to Copy pane to the folder or card selected in the Music on Device pane.

When Windows Media Player finishes copying the marked tracks, they appear in the list shown in the Music on Device pane. You can then disconnect the handheld device, put on your headphones, and listen to your tunes.

Printing

Although printing is usually performed with a program, such as a word processor or a graphics program, you can print documents directly from the Windows XP desktop. You simply drag the icon for the file you want to print to the shortcut icon for the printer. To create a shortcut to your printer on the desktop, follow these steps:

1. Click the Start button on the Windows taskbar and then click Control Panel in the right-hand column on the Start menu.

2. Click the <u>Printers and Other Hardware</u> hyperlink if the Control Panel window is in Category view. Otherwise, double-click the Printers and Faxes icon if the Control Panel window is in Classic view.

3. If you started the Control Panel in Category view, click the <u>Printers and Faxes</u> hyperlink in the Printers and Other Hardware window. If you started the Control Panel in Classic view, skip this step.

4. Right-click the icon of the printer for which you want to create a shortcut and then click Create Shortcut on the pop-up menu.

5. Click the Yes button in the alert dialog box informing you that Windows can't create a shortcut here and asking you if you want the shortcut created on the desktop instead.

After creating a printer shortcut on the desktop, you can print files stored in folders on your computer by dragging the file icons and then dropping them on top of the printer shortcut. If the file was created by an application such as Word 2003 or Notepad, Windows opens this file in the program and then immediately sends it to the printer. In the case of a graphics file or other type of file not associated with a particular program, Windows just sends the file directly to the printer.

Note that Windows XP lets you know when a document has been successfully sent to the printer by beeping and displaying a message balloon from the printer icon in the Notification area on the Windows taskbar. If this message doesn't automatically disappear from the taskbar, click the balloon to make it go away.

Managing the print queue

Sometimes after sending a bunch of files to a printer, you find that nothing's getting printed, and you need to check out the printer queue to find out what is or is not going on. Because Windows XP supports background printing, a printer queue can get pretty stacked up with print jobs even when everything is proceeding normally.

To check out the print jobs in your printer queue, you need to follow these steps:

1. Open the Printer window with the printer queue by double-clicking the printer shortcut on the Windows desktop.

   If you haven't made such a shortcut, right-click the printer icon in the Notification area (also known as the system tray) on the far-right side of the Windows taskbar and then select Open All Active Printers and Faxes on the pop-up menu that appears.

2. After the window with the print jobs queued up for your printer opens, you can do any of the following things to the contents:

   • To temporarily pause the printing of the documents in the print queue, choose Printer⇨Pause Printing.

   • To remove a particular file from the print queue, select it in the list and then click Document⇨Cancel. To cancel the printing of all the documents, click Printer⇨Cancel All Documents instead.

   • To change the position of a document in the print queue, drag the print queue description to a new position in the list (you can tell where the print job will appear by the appearance of the dark I-beam at the mouse pointer). Note that you can't move a print job to a new position in the queue if the document status shows that the job is currently being printed.

3. After you finish reviewing and changing the settings for the jobs in the print queue, click the Close box on the printer window.

Installing a new printer

The day may come when you finally get the boss to spring for that new color laser printer. Before you can use that beauty, however, you have to install it by adding the new printer to your Printers folder, using the Add Printer Wizard.

When installing a new printer with the Add Printer Wizard, you can choose to add a local printer (that is, one that's directly cabled to your computer through one of the ports) or a network printer (that is, a printer that's connected to your network with an Ethernet connection, just as your computer is connected to the LAN).

To install a new local printer with the Add Printer Wizard, follow these steps:

1. Click the Start button on the Windows taskbar and then click Control Panel on the right side of the Start menu.

2. Click the <u>Printers and Other Hardware</u> hyperlink if the Control Panel window is in Category view. Otherwise, double-click the Printers and Faxes icon if the Control Panel window is in Classic view.

3. Click the <u>Add a Printer</u> hyperlink in the Printers and Other Hardware window to start the Add Printer Wizard and then click the Next button or press Enter to advance to the Local Printer or Printer Connection dialog box.

4. Make sure that the Add Printer Wizard selects the Local Printer radio button and the Automatically Detect and Install My Plug and Play Printer check box beneath this radio button before you click the Next button.

5. If the wizard is unable to detect your printer in the New Printer Detection dialog box, click Next to install the printer manually.

6. Select the port for the printer to use in the Use the Following Port drop-down list box in the Select a Printer Port dialog box and then click the Next button.

7. Click the manufacturer and the model of the printer in the Manufacturers and Printers list boxes, respectively, of the Install Printer Software dialog box. If you have a disk with the software for the printer, put it into your floppy or CD-ROM drive and then click the Have Disk button: Select the drive that contains this disk in the Copy Manufacturer's Files drop-down list box and then click OK.

8. Click the Next button to advance to the Name Your Printer dialog box. If you want, edit the name for the printer in the Printer Name text box. If you want to make the printer that you're installing the default printer that is automatically used whenever you print from Windows or from within a Windows program, leave the Yes radio button selected beneath the heading "Do you want your Windows-based programs to use this printer as the default printer?"

9. Click the Next button to advance to the Printer Sharing dialog box. If you want to share this printer with other users on the network, click the Share Name radio button and then, if you want, edit the share name (this is the name that the other users on the network see when they go to select this printer for printing their documents) that the wizard gives the printer in the Share Name text box.

10. To print a test page from your newly installed printer, click the Yes radio button selected beneath the heading "Would you like to print a test page?" in the Print Test Page dialog box.

11. Click the Next button to advance to the Completing the Add Printer Wizard dialog box, where you can review the settings for your new printer before you click the Finish button or press Enter to finish installing the new printer.

To use the Add Printer Wizard to install a printer that's available through your Local Area Network, you follow just slightly different steps:

1. Click the Start button on the Windows taskbar and then click Control Panel on the right side of the Start menu.

2. Click the <u>Printers and Other Hardware</u> hyperlink if the Control Panel window is in Category view. Otherwise, double-click the Printers and Faxes icon if the Control Panel window is in Classic view.

3. Click the <u>Add a Printer</u> hyperlink in the Printers and Other Hardware window to start the Add Printer Wizard and then click the Next button or press Enter to advance to the Local or Network Printer dialog box.

4. Click the A Network Printer or a Printer Attached to Another Computer radio button in the Local or Network Printer dialog box and then click the Next button or press Enter to the Specify a Printer dialog box.

5. If you know the name of the network printer, click the Connect to This Printer (or to Browse for a Printer, Select This Option and Click Next) radio button and then enter the network path in the Name text box. If your network printer is on a network that uses an Internet address, and you know this URL, click the Connect to a Printer on the Internet or on a Home or Office Network radio button and then enter the address in the URL text box. If you know neither of these pieces of information, leave the Browse for a Printer radio button selected and then click Next to advance to the Browse for Printer dialog box.

6. In the Browse for Printer dialog box, locate the printer in the Shared Printers list box by clicking the network icons until you expand the outline sufficiently to display the printer icon. When you click the printer icon in this outline, the wizard adds the path to the Printer text box above.

7. Click the Next button to advance the Default Printer dialog box. If you want to make the printer that you're installing the default printer that is automatically used whenever you print from Windows or from within a Windows program, leave the Yes radio button selected beneath the heading "Do you want your Windows-based programs to use this printer as the default printer?"

8. Click the Next button to advance to the Completing the Add Printer Wizard dialog box, where you can review the settings for your new printer before you click the Finish button or press Enter to finish installing the new printer.

After you add a printer to your computer, you can start using it when printing with programs such as Word 2003 and Excel 2003 or when printing from Windows itself.

 To switch to a new printer that you haven't designated as the default printer in programs such as Word and Excel, you need to open the Print dialog box (choose File⇨Print) and then select the printer name in the Name drop-down list box.

Searching for Files and Folders

The Search feature enables you to quickly locate all those misplaced files that you're just sure are hiding somewhere on your hard drive.

To open the Search Results window to search for a file, follow these steps:

1. Click the Start button on the taskbar and then click Search on the right side of the Start menu. This action opens the Search Results window.

2. Click the All Files and Folders hyperlink in the Search Companion Explorer bar on the left side of the Search Results window.

3. Enter the name of the file or folder in the All or Part of the File Name text box in the Search Companion Explorer bar.

   If you're not entirely sure of the file or folder name, enter the characters you're sure of, followed by the * wildcard character. Windows will then search for all files that begin with the characters you entered, regardless of what letters or characters follow.

4. (Optional) If you remember a keyword or phrase that might help in locating the file or folder, click the A Word or Phrase in the File text box, and enter the text there.

5. By default, Windows searches the main hard drive of your computer for the file. To have Windows search a different drive on your system, click the Look In drop-down button, and click the name of the drive in the pop-up menu.

6. (Optional) You can narrow the search by indicating the approximate date when the file or folder was created. To do this, click the When Was It Modified hyperlink continuation button (two greater-than signs pointing down) and then click the appropriate radio button: Within the Last Week, Past

Month, Within the Past Year, or Specify Dates. When you click the Specify Dates radio button, the From and To text boxes become active so that you can enter the starting and ending date for the time period.

7. (Optional) You can narrow the search by indicating the approximate size of the file or folder. To do this, click the What Size Is It continuation button (two greater-than signs pointing down) and then click the appropriate radio button: Small (Less Than 100 KB), Medium (Less Than 1 MB), Large (More Than 1 MB), or Specify Size. When you click the Specify Size radio button, you can specify the minimum or maximum size, in kilobytes, by entering the lowest or highest number of KB in the Specify Size text box. By default, Windows uses the value you enter as the minimum size (indicated by the appearance of At Least in the associated drop-down list box). To designate the value as the maximum size, click the drop-down button to the right of At Least, and click At Most in the pop-up menu.

8. (Optional) By default, Windows searches the system folders and all subfolders within the designated drive. To prevent Windows from searching these places, or to have Windows search hidden files and folders, specify a case-sensitive search, or search a tape backup drive connected to your system, click the More Advanced Options continuation button (two greater-than signs pointing down) and then clear the check box for the search options you don't want used (Search System Folders, and Search Subfolders). To have Windows search for hidden files and folders, click the Search Hidden Files and Folders check box. To have Windows conduct a case-sensitive search for the filename, click the Case Sensitive check box to put a check mark in it. To have Windows search a tape backup drive, click the Search Tape Backup check box to give it a check mark.

9. (Optional) To narrow the search to only files of a particular type on the designated drive, click the Type of File drop-down button in the More Advanced Options section and then click the type of file to search for in the drop-down list.

10. Click the Search button at the bottom of the Search Companion Explorer bar to start the search. If the file or folder you're searching for appears in the right pane of the Search Results window before the search is completed, or you see that you're getting completely wrong results, click the Stop button.

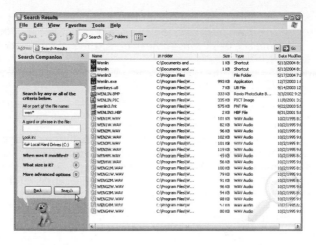

When Windows XP completes a search, it displays a list of all the files and folders that meet your search conditions in the right pane of the Search Results window (as shown in the preceding figure). This list includes the file or folder name, location, size, type, and the date the file or folder was last modified.

If the list contains the file you wanted, you can open a window on the folder that contains the file by right-clicking that icon and then clicking Open on the shortcut menu.

If you didn't find the file or folder you were looking for, and you want to continue your search, you can click the <u>Change File Name or Keywords</u> hyperlink in the Search Companion Explorer bar or the <u>Look in More Locations</u> hyperlink and refine these search criteria. To start a new search, click the Start a New Search button instead.

Searching for computers, people, and Web sites

Files aren't the only things that you can search for with the Search command. In addition, you click the <u>Computers or People</u> hyperlink in the Search Companion Explorer bar of the Search Results window to search for computers on your network or people in your address book.

To find a computer on your local area network, click the <u>A Computer on the Network</u> hyperlink under the heading "What are you looking for." Enter the name of the computer in the Computer Name text box that appears before you click the Search button.

When you search for people, Windows normally searches in your e-mail address book (**see** "Adding Contacts" in Part II for details).

You can also search online directories, such as the Bigfoot Internet Directory Service or the VeraSign Internet Directory Service. To do an online search using one of these directories, click the drop-down button attached to the Look In drop-down list box (which currently reads Address Book), and select the directory to search in the pop-up menu. Enter the name of the person you're trying to locate, along with his or her e-mail address, in the appropriate text boxes and then click the Find Now button to begin the search.

Note that when you search one of the online directories, such as Bigfoot, Windows connects you to that directory on the Internet before beginning the search. After Windows finishes searching the Address Book or online directory, the results of the search appear at the bottom of an expanded Find People dialog box.

To search for someone listed in your address book, follow these steps:

1. Click the People in Your Address Book hyperlink in the Search Companion Explorer bar to open the Find People dialog box.

2. Enter either the name or the e-mail address of the person you want to find in the appropriate text box.

   Note that when you search the address book, you can also search for the person by his or her mailing address, telephone number, or some comment that you've entered about the person.

3. Click the Find Now button to begin searching your Address Book or the online directory you selected.

4. When you finish your people-searching, click the Close button in the upper-right corner of the Find People dialog box.

To search for Web sites on the Internet, you click the Search the Internet hyperlink in the Search Companion Explorer bar. Then type keywords or a phrase indicating the kind of sites you want to find in the What Are You Looking For text box (such as **Caribbean vacations**) and then click the Search button.

Windows then connects you to the Internet and displays the search results on the MSN Web Search page (which appears within the Search Results window to the right of the Search Companion Explorer bar). To browse one of the links on this site, scroll to it and then click it with the mouse. For more information on searching the Internet, *see* "Searching the Web" in Part II.

Searching for pictures, music, or video

The Windows XP search feature lets you restrict your file search to picture or photographic files, sound files, or video files. To search for files containing these kinds of media, you open the Search Results window (by clicking Start and then clicking Search) and then click the <u>Pictures, Music, or Video</u> hyperlink at the top of the Search Companion Explorer bar on the left side of the window.

Click the check box for the type of files (Pictures and Photos, Music, or Video) that you're looking for and then enter the complete or partial filename in the All or Part of the Filename text box below. Remember that you can use the wildcard characters ? (for single missing characters) and * (for multiple missing characters) when entering the name of the file(s) to locate. After you finish selecting the type of files to locate and the name of the file(s) to locate, click the Search button. Windows then lists all the files of the specified type that match the specified filename on the right side of the Search Results window.

Selecting Commands on Menus

Menus provide the means for Windows to organize and display the command choices you have at any given time, as well as the means for you to indicate your particular command choice.

Windows XP relies mainly on three types of command menus (each of which I describe more fully in the following sections):

- ✔ Pull-down menus that are attached to the menu bar that appears along the top of the window.

- ✔ Shortcut menus (sometimes known as context menus) that are attached to a particular object, such as the Windows desktop, the Windows taskbar, or the Recycle Bin icon.

- ✔ Control menus that are attached to the program or document icon that appears in the very upper-left corner of the program or application window.

The following are a few general guidelines that apply when using these types of menus:

- ✔ If you see a right-facing black triangle to the right of an item on a menu, another submenu or submenus containing more options appears when you highlight (or select) that item.

- ✔ If you see an ellipsis (. . .) at the end of a menu item, a dialog box appears when you select that option; **see** "Dialog boxes" later in this section.

- ✔ If you don't see any kind of symbol next to a menu item, the selected option is carried out immediately.

Pull-down menus

Pull-down menus are the primary means for making your wishes known in Windows XP. (Although most commands on pull-down menus live up to their names and appear below the menu, some, such as the Start menu, actually display their options above the menu name when you open them.)

Within windows such as My Documents, My Computer, Windows Explorer, and Internet Explorer 6, the pull-down menus are located on the menu bars right below the title bar.

Three methods used to open pull-down menus and select commands are:

✔ **Using the mouse:** Point to the pull-down menu (a "shadowed" button appears) and then click the menu name on the menu bar to open the menu. Move the mouse pointer through the menu to highlight the desired command and then click to select the menu command.

✔ **Using the Alt key:** Press the Alt key to display the command letter (also known as the hot key and shown by underlining) in the menu or menu item name (the command letter is the one that's underlined in the name). Continue to hold down the Alt key as you type the command letter in the menu name to open the pull-down menu. Then type the command letter of the menu item to select the command.

✔ **Using the F10 function key:** Press the F10 key to activate the menu bar (the File menu name becomes a raised button, and the command letters are displayed in the menu names). Either type the command letter in the menu name, or press the → key to highlight the desired menu and use the ↓ key to open the menu. Press the appropriate arrow key to navigate until the desired menu item is highlighted and then press the Enter key to select it. Note that after a pull-down menu is open, you can use the ↓ or → key to select and open other pull-down menus on the menu bar.

To open the Start menu on the Windows taskbar with the keyboard, press Ctrl+Esc. If you want to see the underlined command letters for navigating Windows menus and dialog boxes at all times, follow these steps:

 1. Right-click the Windows desktop and then click Properties on the shortcut menu.

 2. Click the Appearance tab in the Display Properties dialog box.

 3. Click the Effects button in the Display Properties dialog box to open the Effects dialog box.

4. Click the Hide Underlined Letters for Keyboard Navigation Until I Press the Alt Key check box to remove that check mark and then click the OK button.

Shortcut menus

Shortcut (also known as *context*) *menus* are pop-up menus that are attached to particular objects in Windows, such as the desktop icons or even the desktop itself. These menus contain commands directly related to the object to which they're attached.

To open a shortcut menu, right-click the object with the mouse. After you open a shortcut menu, you click the menu item to select it.

Shortcut menus attached to program, folder, and file icons on the desktop or in a window usually contain varying assortments of the following commands:

- ✔ **Open:** Opens the file or folder.

- ✔ **Send To:** Sends a copy of the file or folder to such places as the Desktop (Create Shortcut), Compressed (Zipped) Folder (*see* "Compressing files and folders" earlier in this part), Infrared Recipient (that is, another computer or printer that's connected by an infrared port), Mail Recipient, My Documents, or Share-to-Web Upload Folder (to put on your Web site).

- ✔ **Cut, Copy and Paste:** Cuts or copies the file or folder to the Clipboard so that it can be moved or copied to another place on your system or network by selecting the Paste command. *See* "Copying (and Moving) Files and Folders" earlier in this part for more on this topic.

- ✔ **Create Shortcut:** Creates a shortcut to the selected file or folder. *See* "Creating Shortcuts" earlier in this part for details.

- ✔ **Delete:** Deletes the file or folder by putting it into the Recycle Bin. *See* "Deleting Junk" earlier in this part for details.

- ✔ **Rename:** Changes the name of the selected object. *See* "Renaming files and folders" earlier in this part for details.

- ✔ **Properties:** Gives the lowdown on the selected file or folder. For details, *see* "Getting Info on a Disk, Folder, or File" earlier in this part.

Dialog boxes

Most dialog boxes appear as a result of selecting a menu command from either a pull-down menu or a shortcut menu. You can always tell when choosing a command will open a dialog box, because the command name is followed by an ellipsis (that's Greek for three dots in a row).

For example, you know that choosing the Options . . . command on the Tools pull-down menu in a Windows XP window opens an Options dialog box, because the command appears as Options . . . (with the ellipsis) rather than as Options (no ellipsis).

At the top of each dialog box, you find a title bar that contains the name of the dialog box. You can reposition the dialog box on the screen by dragging it by the title bar (and nowhere else). You can't, however, resize a dialog box, which is the major difference between a dialog box and a window.

Dialog boxes also contain any number of buttons and boxes that you use to make your selections known to Windows XP or to the particular Windows program you have open. The following figure points out many of the various boxes and buttons you encounter in dialog boxes. The following table tells you how to use the boxes and buttons.

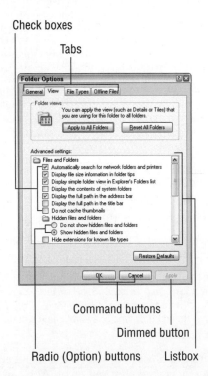

Check boxes

Tabs

Command buttons

Dimmed button

Radio (Option) buttons   Listbox

Parts of a Dialog Box	*What You Do with Them*
Check box	Used with items that enable you to choose more than one option. Selected options appear with a check mark inside the box, whereas the current check-box option appears with a faint, dotted line around the option name.
Command button	Used to initiate an action, such as putting the options you've selected into effect by clicking the OK button.
Dimmed button	If the command name is dimmed, the button is temporarily out of commission — until you select another prerequisite option.
Drop-down list box	Looks like a text box with a down-arrow button right next door. Click the drop-down button to open a list box of possible choices. If more choices than will fit in the box are available, use the scroll bar on the right to display more choices.
List box	Displays an alphabetical list of all choices for an item. Use the scroll bar on the right to display new choices. The current choice is highlighted in the list.
Radio (Option) button	Used with items when you can choose only one of several options. The selected option appears with a dot in the middle of the radio button and a faint dotted line around the option name.
Slider	Enables you to change a value (such as the sound playback volume or mouse speed) by dragging the slider back and forth (usually between Low and High, marked at each end).
Spinner button	Enables you to select a new number in an accompanying edit box without having to actually type in that box. Clicking the up-arrow spinner button increases the value by one, and clicking the down-arrow spinner button decreases it by one.
Tab	Lets you select a new page of options in the same dialog box, complete with their own buttons and boxes.
Text box	Shows you the current setting, and enables you to edit it or type in a whole new setting. If the text inside the box is selected, anything you type replaces the highlighted text. You can also delete text by pressing the Delete or Backspace key.

Note that if the name on a command button is followed by an ellipsis (. . .), clicking the button displays another dialog box. However, if the name of a command button is followed by two greater-than symbols (>), choosing the button expands the current dialog box to display more choices.

After you use these various buttons and boxes to make changes to the current settings controlled by the dialog box, you can close the dialog box and put the new settings into effect by choosing the OK button. If you want to close the dialog box without making *any* changes to the current settings, press the Esc key or click the Close button of the dialog box (the button with the X in it, located in the very upper-right corner of the dialog box).

Alert dialog boxes

An *alert dialog box* is a special type of dialog box that appears whenever Windows XP can't perform a prescribed task or when you're in a program and about to engage in an activity with possibly dire consequences. All alert dialog boxes basically say, "You can't get there from here." Click the OK button to clear the dialog box and then start whatever process didn't work all over again (after taking care of the problem that Windows was complaining about). Click the Yes button (if the dialog box has one) to agree with the suggestion, or click the No button to leave things as they are.

Wizards

Wizards are a series of dialog boxes designed specifically to walk you through some sort of setup, such as installing a new printer or creating a new dial-up connection for getting online via your modem.

Many times, you will know that you're dealing with a wizard because the title of the initial dialog box says something like "Accessibility Settings Wizard" or "Add Printer Wizard". Other times, the title bar of the initial wizard dialog box doesn't use the term *wizard* at all.

Even when the title bar doesn't give you any indication, you can still tell that you're dealing with a wizard because of the characteristic Back and Next buttons at the bottom of the dialog boxes. Also, you can tell when you've reached the last wizard dialog box, because this dialog box has a Finish button. As soon as you click this button, Windows closes the dialog box and puts your new settings into effect.

Control menus

The Control menu is a standard pull-down menu attached to all the windows that you'll ever open in Windows XP. To open the Control menu, click the little icon to the immediate left of the window name in the upper-left corner of the window title bar.

If you double-click rather than single-click this icon, Windows closes the window and quits any application program that happens to be running in it. If you have an unsaved document open in the program whose window you just closed, Windows XP displays an alert dialog box that gives you a chance to save it before shutting down the shop. **See** "Alert dialog boxes" earlier in this section.

Almost every Control menu you run into has these soon-to-become-old-hat commands on it:

Common Menu Commands	What They Do
Restore	Restores a maximized or minimized window to an in-between size that you can easily change
Move	Moves the window to a new location on the desktop
Size	Enables you to resize the window by moving the left, right, top, or bottom side
Minimize	Shrinks the window all the way down to a button on the taskbar at the bottom of the screen
Maximize	Zooms the window to full size so that it fills up the entire screen
Close (Alt+F4)	Closes the window, thus automatically exiting the program running in it

Selecting Commands on Explorer Bars

Explorer bars are a special type of command bar that's featured prominently in windows such as the My Documents, My Computer, Windows Explorer, and the Internet Explorer 6 windows. When you open an Explorer bar in a window, the Explorer pane appears to the immediate left of the window, replacing the navigation pane, subdividing the window into two panes: Explorer on the far left and the main part of the window on the right.

Windows XP offers several different types of Explorer bars (many of which are Internet-related). To display a particular Explorer bar, click View⇨Explorer Bar on the window menu bar and then select one of the following commands from the submenu that appears:

- ✔ **Search:** (Ctrl+E) Opens or closes the Search Companion Explorer bar so that you can search for files, people, or for Web sites on the Internet; **see** "Searching for Files and Folders" earlier in this part and "Searching the Web" in Part II for details.

✔ **Favorites:** (Ctrl+I) Opens or closes the Favorites Explorer bar, which contains a list of hyperlinks to your favorite Web sites, folders, and files. Use the hyperlinks on the Favorites Explorer bar to revisit one of the Web sites on the Internet or to open a favorite local folder or file; *see* "Adding Web Favorites" in Part II for details on adding stuff.

✔ **History:** (Ctrl+H) Opens or closes the History Explorer bar, which contains a chronological list of hyperlinks to Web sites that you've recently visited and the folders and files that you've recently opened. Use the hyperlinks on the History Explorer bar to revisit Web sites on the Internet or to reopen a local folder or file.

✔ **Research:** Opens or closes the Research pane in the window. When the Research pane is open, Windows searches online resources such as the Encarta dictionary and MSN Search, among others, for words and phrases that you enter in the Search For text box when you click the Start Searching button (the green one with the white arrow pointing to the right).

✔ **Folders:** Opens or closes the Folders pane in the window. When the Folders pane is open, you can open any of the objects that make up your computer system, such as the folders and files on particular disk drives in the pane on the right; *see* "Browsing Drives, Folders, and Files on the Computer" earlier in this part for more information.

✔ **Tip of the Day:** Opens and closes a Did You Know pane at the bottom of the window where you can peruse a group of short how-to tips on better ways to perform common tasks in Windows XP.

✔ **Discuss:** To open and close the Comments pane at the bottom of the main section of the window, where comments are made by participants in an online discussion.

 You can also open and close the Search and Folders Explorer bars by clicking the appropriate buttons (Search and Folders) on the Standard Buttons toolbar. Note also that you can close any Explorer bar by clicking the Close button (the one with the X).

Selecting Commands from Toolbars

Toolbars (often shortened to *bars*) contain the buttons and menus that you use to get things done. Different types of toolbars (each with its own group of buttons) appear within the various folder windows, such as My Documents, Windows Explorer, and My Computer, the Web browsing window opened by Internet Explorer 6, as well as on the taskbar on the Windows XP desktop.

When you first display toolbars in a window, they appear docked, one on top of the other, in neat little rows at the top of the window. When you first display toolbars on the taskbar, they appear one after the other on the taskbar, often scrunching up the buttons representing the various windows open on the desktop and with spinner buttons for displaying new groups of buttons.

To display a certain type of toolbar in one of the folder windows, such as My Documents, Windows Explorer, or My Computer, click View⇨Toolbars on the window menu bar and then select one of the following commands on the cascading menu that appears:

✓ **Standard Buttons:** Displays or hides the Standard Buttons toolbar. The particular buttons that appear on this toolbar depend on whether you're browsing local files and folders or Web pages on the Internet or the corporate intranet.

✓ **Address Bar:** Displays or hides the Address bar, which contains a text box in which you can enter the URL of the Web page you want to visit or the pathname of the folders you want to browse.

✓ **Links:** Displays or hides the Links bar, which contains buttons with links to your favorite Web pages.

✓ **Lock the Toolbars:** When this menu item is selected (indicated by a check mark in front of the name), you can't undock the toolbars that appear in the window (in other words, they're frozen in place).

✓ **Customize:** Displays the Customize Toolbar dialog box, where you can customize the current toolbar by adding, deleting, and/or rearranging the buttons.

Note that if installed other programs that offer their own toolbars (such as Adobe PDF), their toolbars will appear on this list as well.

To display a certain type of toolbar on the Windows XP taskbar, right-click the taskbar (making sure that you don't click the Start button or any of the other buttons that currently appear on the taskbar), select Toolbars on the shortcut menu, and choose one of the following commands on the cascading menu that appears:

✓ **Address:** Displays or hides the Address Bar, which contains a text box in which you can enter the URL of the Web page you want to visit or the pathname of the folders you want to browse.

Windows Media Player: Displays Windows Media Player's playback controls on a button on the taskbar when Windows Media Player's window is minimized.

✓ **Links:** Displays or hides the Links bar, which contains buttons with links to favorite Web pages.

✔ **Language Bar:** Displays or Hides the Language-Bar icon in the navigation area on the right side of the Windows taskbar when you use an Office XP program, such as Word 2003 or Excel 2003. To display the Language Bar on-screen so that you can use the Dictation, Voice Command, or Handwriting features, click the Language-Bar icon on the taskbar and then click the Show Language Bar option on the pop-up menu.

✔ **Desktop:** Hides or displays the Desktop toolbar, which contains buttons for all the icons you have on your desktop.

✔ **Quick Launch:** Displays or hides the Quick Launch toolbar, which contains buttons for launching Internet Explorer 6 and Outlook Express, along with a Show Desktop button for minimizing all open windows to show only the Windows XP desktop.

✔ **New Toolbar:** Opens the New Toolbar dialog box, where you can make the items in a particular folder into buttons on a new custom toolbar.

If the taskbar is already full of buttons, and you don't have much leeway for opening the taskbar shortcut menu with the Toolbars command, you can always right-click somewhere on the time in the Notification area of the taskbar (at the far right side where the current time is displayed) to do so. Right-clicking the current time in the Notification area always brings up the shortcut menu for the taskbar, whereas right-clicking a button that appears on the taskbar or an icon in the status area opens a shortcut menu for just that button or icon.

The Address Bar

You can use the Address Bar to search or browse Web pages on the Internet or your corporate intranet, or to browse folders and files on local or networked disk drives. Just click the Address Bar to insert the cursor into the text, type in the URL of the Web page or the pathname of the folder you want to browse and then press the Enter key.

If you add the Address Bar to the Windows XP taskbar and then use it to browse a local drive or folder or Web page on the Internet, the folders and files appear in a full-screen version of the My Computer window, and the Web pages appear in a full-screen version of Internet Explorer 6.

If you use the Address Bar in My Computer, Windows Explorer, or in the Internet Explorer 6 window (where the Address Bar is automatically displayed) to browse local drives or folders or Internet Web pages, the folders, files, or Web pages appear in the particular window in whatever size it currently assumes.

See also "Browsing Drives, Folders, and Files on the Computer" earlier in this part and "Searching the Web," both in Part II, for more information on using the Address Bar.

The Desktop toolbar

The Desktop toolbar contains buttons for all the icons that appear on the Windows XP desktop (or, if there's insufficient room, a Desktop button that, when clicked, displays a pop-up menu of items). These buttons or menu items include such things as My Documents to display the My Documents window, My Network Places to display the My Network Places window, Internet Explorer to launch the Internet Explorer, and Recycle Bin to open the Recycle Bin window. Along with these standard buttons or items, this toolbar contains ones for all the desktop shortcuts you add for opening programs, folders, and files; *see* "Creating Shortcuts" earlier in this part for more information on shortcuts.

By displaying the Desktop toolbar, you retain access to the desktop icons even when you remove their display from the desktop. Remember that you can hide and then redisplay the desktop icons by right-clicking the desktop and then clicking Arrange Icons By⇨Show Desktop Icons on the shortcut menus.

The Links toolbar

The buttons on the Links toolbar (more often than not called simply the *Links bar*) are hyperlinks that open favorite Web pages (or, if you lack sufficient room on the taskbar, a Links button that, when clicked, opens a menu of hyperlinks to these pages). When you first start using Windows XP, the Links bar contains only buttons or items with links to Web pages on the Microsoft Web site. These include the following:

- ✔ **Customize Links** opens a page with tips on how to add buttons to the Links bar.

- ✔ **Free Hotmail** opens the MSN Hotmail page, where you can sign up for a free Hotmail e-mail address.

- ✔ **Windows** opens a page with the latest information about Windows XP.

- ✔ **Windows Media** opens the WindowsMedia.com page, where you can listen to the latest music or download the latest John Mayer or Liz Phair video.

You can, if you want, add to the Links toolbar custom buttons that open your favorite Web pages or preferred folders and files that reside on your desktop. To add a button with a link to a preferred Web page, folder, or file, you simply drag that icon to the place on the Links bar where you want it to appear (this icon appears on the Address Bar in front of the Web-page URL or folder or file pathname). You can tell where the new button will appear, because a dark I-beam appears at the place where the button will be inserted when you release the mouse button.

To delete a button that you no longer want on the Links bar, rightclick the button and then choose the Delete command on the button shortcut menu.

The menu bar

The menu bar in folder windows, such as My Documents, My Computer, Windows Explorer, and the Web browser window of Internet Explorer 6, all contain the pull-down menus that you use to perform all kinds of routine tasks. These windows contain the following menus:

- ✔ **File:** Does file-type stuff, such as renaming or deleting files and folders or creating shortcuts to them.

- ✔ **Edit:** Does editing-type stuff, such as cutting, copying, or pasting files or folders.

- ✔ **View:** Does show-and-tell stuff, such as displaying or hiding particular toolbars or parts of the window and changing the way file and folder icons appear in the windows.

- ✔ **Favorites:** Adds to, opens, or organizes the folders, files, Web pages, and Web channels that you bookmark or subscribe to.

- ✔ **Tools:** Changes various option settings for the window, such as Folder Options, that determine how you open files and folder icons, what file information is displayed, and which applications open what types of files.

- ✔ **Help:** Consults particular help topics that direct you in how to use Windows XP.

See also "Pull-down menus" earlier in this part for details on using the pull-down menus that you find on the Windows menu bars.

The Standard Buttons toolbar

The Standard Buttons toolbar is the main toolbar that appears in folder windows, such as My Documents, Windows Explorer, and My Computer, as well as in the Internet Explorer 6 window. The buttons on the Standard Buttons toolbar change, depending upon whether you're browsing local folders and files or Web pages on the Internet. When you open one of the folder windows to browse local folders and files, the Standard Buttons toolbar contains the following buttons:

✔ **Back:** Returns to the previously browsed folder or Web page.

✔ **Forward:** Returns to the folder or Web page that you browsed right before using the Back button to return to the current page.

✔ **Up:** Moves up one level in the directory structure.

✔ **Search:** Displays the Search Companion Explorer bar for searching for files, folders, people in your address book, and Web sites on the Internet. *See* "Selecting Commands on Explorer Bars" earlier in this part for details.

✔ **Folders:** Displays the Folders Explorer bar for locating files or folders on your computer. *See* "Selecting Commands on Explorer Bars" earlier in this part for details.

✔ **View:** Click repeatedly to change view options for the icons in the main display of the window. *See* "Arranging and Sizing Icons in a Window" earlier in this part for details on the various view options.

When you browse a Web page, whether it's a local HTML document on your hard drive or one located on a Web server somewhere in cyberspace, the Back and Forward buttons that you see when browsing local folders and files are then joined by the following additional buttons:

✔ **Stop:** Immediately halts the downloading of a Web page that is just taking far too long to come in.

✔ **Refresh:** Refreshes the display of the current Web page (which sometimes helps when the contents of the page appear jumbled or incomplete).

✔ **Home:** Displays the Web page designated as the start page. This Web page appears each time you launch Internet Explorer 6 and connect to the Internet.

✔ **Search:** Displays the Search Companion Explorer bar, which you can use to search for Web sites on the Internet (*see* "Searching the Web" in Part II for details).

✔ **Favorites:** Displays the Favorites Explorer bar for opening files or folders or revisiting favorite Web pages that you've bookmarked.

✔ **Media:** Displays an Explorer bar that contains the controls for playing music and video, along with links from Windows Media.com to featured music artists, movie previews, and online radio stations.

✔ **History:** Displays the History Explorer bar for reopening recently accessed files or folders or revisiting Web pages that you've visited within the last few days or weeks.

✔ **Mail:** Displays a pop-up menu of e-mail options, including Read Mail, New Message, Send a Link, Send Page, and Read News.

✔ **Print:** Sends the current Web page to your printer.

✔ **Edit or Edit with Microsoft Office Word:** Opens the current Web page editor (exposing the *raw* HTML tags), Word in many cases; you can also select the program in which to open the HTML page from the pop-up menu.

The status bar

The folder windows that you routinely use, such as My Documents, My Pictures, My Computer, Windows Explorer, and the like, don't normally display their status bars. To display the status bar for the particular window that you have open, you need to click View⇨ Status Bar on that window's menu bar.

The status bar, when displayed, appears at the bottom of the window, where it gives you statistics, such as the number of objects (that is, drive, folder, and file icons) that the window contains, the size of the objects in kilobytes (KB) or megabytes (MB), plus the name of the parent folder open in the window. When you select a file icon in the window, the status bar gives you specific information on the selected document, including the file type, the date and time it was last modified, and the size.

When you click a folder, the status bar either gives you a rather nondescript, "1 objects selected" message or displays a general description of the folder. For example, when you click the My Music folder in the My Documents window, the status bar displays the message "Stores and manages music files."

 You can always get information about the folder or file you select in a window (whether or not the status bar is displayed) by clicking the Details button in the window navigation pane (the one with the two greater-than signs pointing downward). Clicking this button expands the Details section of the navigation pane to give information on the selected folder or file, such as the size; the date and time last modified; and, in the case of files, the type and author. To shrink the Details section and hide this information in the navigation pane, click the Details button a second time (this time, the icon shows two arrows pointing upward).

Resizing and moving toolbars

The toolbars that appear in the folder windows you open are automatically locked in place. If you want to be able to resize the toolbars to display more or less buttons or to move them to new rows at the top of the window, you must first unlock them. To do this, you right-click one of the toolbars (like the menu bar or the Standard buttons toolbar) and then click Lock the Toolbars on the shortcut menu to remove the check mark from this item.

As soon as you do this, a sizing handle that looks like a separator made up of dots rather than a vertical line appears at the beginning of each toolbar displayed in the open window. You can then move the toolbar to a new row at the top of the window and resize toolbars that share a row by dragging the toolbar by the sizing handle. After you finish repositioning and resizing the toolbars at the top of the window, you can lock them into their new positions by once more right-clicking one of the toolbars and then clicking Lock the Toolbars on the shortcut menu (to add a check mark to this item).

Customizing the Standard Buttons toolbar

You can customize the appearance of the Standard Buttons toolbar in one of the folder windows or the Internet Explorer 6 Web browsing window. In customizing a toolbar, you can change which buttons are displayed and the order in which they appear on the toolbar.

To customize a Standard Buttons toolbar, select View⇨Toolbars⇨ Customize on the window menu bar, or right-click the toolbar and then click the Customize item on the shortcut menu to open the Customize Toolbar dialog box, shown in the following figure.

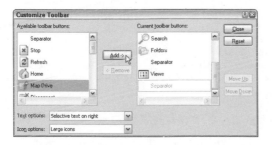

The Customize Toolbar dialog box is divided into sections: the Available Toolbar Buttons list box on the left and the Current Toolbar Buttons list box on the right. To add a button to the Standard Buttons toolbar, you click it in the Available Toolbar Buttons list box and then click the Add button. To remove a button from the toolbar, you click the button in the Current Toolbar Buttons list box and then click the Remove button.

To move a button forward toward the beginning of the Standard Buttons toolbar, you click the button in the Current Toolbar Buttons list box and then click the Move Up button until the button moves up to the desired position. To move a button backward toward the end of the toolbar, click the button in the Current Toolbar Buttons list box and then click the Move Down button until the button moves back to the desired position.

To insert a vertical line separator (used to group buttons) in front of a button on the Standard Buttons toolbar, click the button in the Current Toolbar Buttons list box, click Separator at the very top of the Available Toolbar Buttons list box, and then click the Add button.

In addition to adding, deleting, and moving buttons on the Standard Buttons toolbar, you can change how the buttons are labeled and what size icons are used:

✔ **Text Options:** By default, Windows selectively labels certain buttons (such as Search and Folders) by placing the name to the right of the icon. To have all the buttons so labeled, click Show Text Labels in the Text Options pop-up list. To have none of the buttons labeled, click No Text Labels in this pop-up list.

✔ **Icon Options:** By default, Windows uses large icons for all buttons on the Standard Buttons toolbar. To switch to small icons (so that you can fit more buttons on the bar), click Small Icons in the Icon Options pop-up list.

When you've finished customizing the Standard Buttons toolbar, click the Close button to close the Customize Toolbar dialog box and return to the open window with your customized Standard Buttons toolbar.

 You can always restore the Standard Buttons toolbar to its original state by opening the Customize Toolbar dialog box and then clicking the Reset button before you click Close.

Selecting Files and Folders

To select the files and folders to which you want to do stuff like copy, move, open, or print, you select those icons (the small pictures identifying the folder or file). Most of the time, you click the file and folder icons in the windows to select them. Windows lets you know when an icon is selected by highlighting it in a reverse color (normally, a dark blue unless you change the Windows appearance settings).

If you change the click options for Windows in the Folder Options dialog box so that single-clicking opens an item (**see** "Opening Files and Folders" earlier in this part for details), instead of clicking a folder or file icon to select it (which succeeds only in opening the item), you just hover the mouse pointer over it.

When you need to select more than one file or folder in a window, you have a choice of things to do:

✔ To select all the icons in a window (this includes all drive, file, and folder icons located within it), choose Edit⇨Select All on the window menu bar or press Ctrl+A.

✔ To select multiple folder or file icons that are located all over the place in the window, hold down the Ctrl key as you click each folder or file icon (the Ctrl key adds individual icons to the selection). Note that if you use single-clicking to open items, you need to hover over each item as you hold down the Ctrl key (no easy feat).

✔ To select a series of folder or file icons that are all next to each other in the window, click the first one in the series and then hold the Shift key as you click the last icon in the series (the Shift key adds all the icons in between the first and last one you click to the selection). Note that if you use single-clicking to open items, you need to hover over the first item until it's selected and then hold the Shift key as you hover over the last icon in the series (and if you think Ctrl+hovering is hard, wait till you try Shift+hovering).

✔ To reverse the icon selection in a window so that all the icons that aren't currently selected become selected and all those that are currently selected become deselected, choose Edit⇨Invert Selection on the window menu bar.

Note that the Invert Selection command is really useful when you want to select all but a few folders or files in a window: First, use one of the aforementioned methods to select the icons of the files you do *not* want selected; then choose Edit⇨Invert Selection. Voilà! All the files in the window are selected except for those few you selected in the first place.

Shutting Down Windows

Windows XP includes a shut-down procedure that you really should follow before you pull the plug on your machine. To shut down Windows XP so that you can safely shut off your computer and get home to the kids or whatever, follow these steps:

1. Click the Start button on the Windows taskbar and then click the Turn Off Computer button that appears at the bottom right of the Start menu to display the Turn Off Computer dialog box.

2. Click the Turn Off button (the red one in the middle with the white vertical bar inside a white circle).

In addition to the Turn Off option, you can select the following two options in the Turn Off Computer dialog box:

✔ **Stand By:** Select Stand By to put your computer into a deep sleep. This mode powers down the computer but maintains the state of your desktop.

✔ **Restart:** Select Restart to shut down and then immediately restart the computer (which you often have to do after installing a new piece of hardware or software, for example). You can also use this option in the unlikely event that Windows XP becomes so screwed up that you need to restart the whole shebang (when, for example, all the colors on the desktop get messed up and go all magenta and green on you).

A couple of notes on using the Turn Off option in the Turn Off Computer dialog box:

✔ Windows XP displays a screen telling you that you can safely turn off the power to your computer. Should you decide that you want to restart the computer at that point, press Ctrl+Alt+Del (the old three-finger salute in DOS!) to restart Windows XP.

✔ When your computer is connected to a LAN, and someone is currently connected to your computer, Windows XP displays a warning dialog box indicating that you're about to disconnect one or more people. Choose OK to go ahead and make these folks mad as all-get-out, or choose Cancel and then find out who's connected and make it his or her responsibility to shut down Windows XP on your computer after he or she logs off (so that you can go home and have a life).

 If you share your computer with other users, you can use the Log Off button (immediately to the left of the Turn Off button at the bottom of the Start menu) to close down your work session without having to shut down the power to the computer (so your co-worker can use the machine to get some work done). To do this, just click the Log Off button in the Log Off Windows dialog box that appears when you click the Log Off button on the Start menu. If you want to let a co-worker use the machine but intend to return to it later yourself, click the Switch User button instead.

Using the Command Prompt

For any of you Windows users who find yourselves longing for the good old days when you used DOS to get things done on a computer, Windows XP enables you to open a window with the DOS command prompt so that you can type away your nostalgia.

Everything you need to know about using the Command Prompt window:

- ✓ To open the Command Prompt window within Windows XP, click the Start button on the taskbar (or press Ctrl+Esc); point to All Programs, followed by Accessories; and then click the Command Prompt on the continuation menu.

- ✓ To return to Windows XP and close the Command Prompt window, type **exit** at the command prompt and then press Enter. You can also close the Command Prompt window by clicking the Close box.

Don't fool around with DOS commands unless you're really sure of what you're doing. If you ever get a DOS window open and then get cold feet, just click the Close button in the Command Prompt window to close it and get back to Windows XP, where you belong.

Using the Windows Taskbar

The taskbar is your constant companion in Windows XP. No matter where you go or what you do, the taskbar and the buttons of the various toolbars continue to be displayed along the bottom of the screen. That way, you have access to all of those features no matter whether you're doing a letter in your favorite word processor, surfing the Web with Internet Explorer 6, or perusing your favorite graphic images in the My Pictures window.

The taskbar forms the base of the Windows XP desktop. Running along the bottom of the complete width of the screen, the taskbar is divided into three sections:

- ✓ **The Start button** with the accompanying Start pop-up menu at the far left

- ✓ **Buttons for open toolbars and minimized windows** in the center area

- ✓ **The Notification area** (at the far right; also called the system tray) with current time and icons showing the current status of computer components and programs and processes that are running in the background

When you open a folder window or program window on the Windows desktop, Windows adds a button representing that window to the center section of the taskbar. When you have multiple windows open at a time, you can bring a window to the top of the stack by clicking that button on the taskbar.

Whenever you minimize a window by clicking the Minimize button, Windows reduces it to just a button on the taskbar. When you click this button on the taskbar, Windows restores the window to the previous size and position on the Windows desktop.

The Start menu

The Start button that opens the Start menu (*see* "Launching Programs" earlier in this part) always appears as the first button on the taskbar. The Start menu is the most basic pull-down menu in Windows XP, containing almost all the commands you'll ever need to use.

To open the Start menu, simply click the Start button in the lower-left corner of the taskbar or press Ctrl+Esc.

The Start menu is divided into two columns, with your user name and picture appearing in the bar at the top of the menu (as you can see, I'm the rubber ducky on our network — *see* "User Accounts" in Part IV for information on how to change your picture) and the Log Off and Turn Off Computer buttons appearing in a bar at the very bottom.

In the right column of the Start menu, the following options are fixed and never change: Help and Support, Search, and Run at the bottom; Control Panel, Set Program Access and Defaults, Connect To, and Printers and Faxes in the middle; and My Documents, My Recent Documents, My Picture, My Music, My Computer, and My Network Places at the top. In the left column, only the All Programs button at the bottom and the E-Mail and Internet options at the top are fixed. All the other icons that appear in the area in between change over time as they represent icons of the programs that you launch most frequently.

To fix a particular option on the Start menu, open the menu and then right-click the option before you click Pin to Start Menu on its shortcut menu.

To open a folder window, such as My Documents or My Network Places, connect to the Internet, get your e-mail, or run one of the recently used programs, you simply click that icon in the Start menu. To display a pop-up continuation menu displaying all the rest of the programs installed on your computer, you click the More Programs button. You can then launch a particular program by clicking that item on the Programs menu.

See "Customizing the taskbar and Start menu" later in this part for details on how you can change the look and contents of the Start menu.

The Quick Launch toolbar

The Quick Launch toolbar adds a group of buttons to the Windows taskbar that you can use to start commonly used modules to get back to the desktop. These buttons may include:

- ✔ **Show Desktop:** Minimizes all open windows in order to obtain immediate access to the Windows Desktop and all the desktop shortcuts and Web items that it contains.

- ✔ **Launch Internet Explorer Browser:** Starts Internet Explorer 6 for browsing Web pages.

- ✔ **Launch Outlook Express:** Starts Outlook Express for sending and receiving e-mail and messages from the newsgroups to which you have subscribed.

- ✔ **Windows Media Player:** Starts Windows Media Player so that you can play music or video on your computer (*see* "Playing Music, Video, and Movies" earlier in this part for details).

In addition to these standard buttons, you can add your own custom buttons to the Quick Launch toolbar by dragging the shortcuts to your favorite program from the desktop or the program file from an open folder window to the Quick Launch toolbar. Follow these steps:

1. Open My Computer or Windows Explorer and then open the folder that contains the executable file that starts the program you want to add to the Quick Launch toolbar or that contains a shortcut to this executable file.

2. Drag the program file icon or shortcut icon to the desired position on the Quick Launch toolbar and then release the mouse button. The mouse pointer indicates where the new button will be inserted with a dark I-beam cursor at the tip of the pointer.

   A button for the program appears at the position of the I-beam in the Quick Launch toolbar.

You can delete any of the buttons from the Quick Launch toolbar by right-clicking the button, clicking the Delete command on the shortcut menu, and then clicking the Yes button in the alert dialog box that asks you to confirm the deletion.

 As you continue to add new buttons to the Quick Launch toolbar, some of the existing buttons at the end of the bar become hidden from view. Windows then adds a continuation button (>) to the end of the Quick Launch toolbar, which you can click to display a pop-up menu with the other options you add.

The Notification area

The Notification area (or system tray) displays the current time and icons that indicate the active status of various components, such as the status of your network connection, Active Sync connection to your handheld device, PCMCIA cards inserted into a laptop computer, or the printer queue. In addition, icons representing various programs or processes that run in the background, such as the Language Bar for using the new Voice Recognition and Handwriting Recognition in Office XP programs, the Windows Clipboard when it contains multiple items, and Windows Messenger.

This is also the place from which the Windows Update feature added to Windows XP displays the annoying Update Reminder message telling you that new updates for the system are available; *see* "Using Windows Automatic Update" later in this part for more on this feature.

To identify an icon that appears in the status area, position the mouse pointer over it until the ScreenTip appears. To change the status of an icon, right-click it to display the pop-up menu and then click the appropriate menu option. For example, to open the Volume Control dialog box to adjust the volume of your speakers, you right-click the speaker icon in the Notification area and then click Open Volume Control on the pop-up menu.

To temporarily expand the Notification area so that all its icons are displayed, click the Show Hidden Icons button (the one to the left of the first displayed icon in this area with an arrowhead pointing to the left). Note that you can also customize the Notification area as part of customizing the taskbar and Start menu properties. *See* "Customizing the Notification area" later in this part for details.

Customizing the Taskbar and Start menu

The Taskbar and Start Menu Properties dialog box enables you to customize the settings for the taskbar and the Start menu. To open this dialog box, right-click the Start button or any open area (with no buttons) on the taskbar and then click Properties on the taskbar shortcut menu and the Taskbar tab in the Taskbar and Start Menu Properties dialog box.

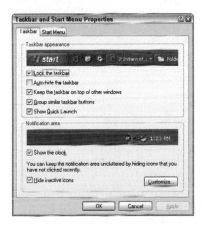

The check boxes in the Taskbar Appearance section at the top of the Taskbar tab in the Taskbar and Start Menu Properties dialog box do the following:

- ✔ **Lock the Taskbar:** Locks all of the bars so that you can't adjust the size of the different areas of the taskbar, such as the Quick Launch toolbar.

- ✔ **Auto-Hide the Taskbar:** Hides the taskbar until you roll the mouse pointer somewhere over that position. This way, the taskbar appears only when you need it.

- ✔ **Keep the Taskbar on Top of Other Windows:** Always places the taskbar in front of any window that you move down so far that they overlap it.

- ✔ **Group Similar Taskbar Buttons:** Displays buttons for files opened by the same program in the same area of the taskbar.

Moreover, if the taskbar becomes so crowded with buttons that become too small to display, Windows collapses the buttons for a particular program into one button that, when clicked, displays a pop-up menu from which you can select the file you want to display on the desktop.

✔ **Show Quick Launch:** Displays the Quick Launch toolbar on the Windows taskbar immediately following the Start button.

Customizing the Notification area

You can also customize the settings for the Notification area of the taskbar by altering the settings in the Notification area section of the Taskbar tab. By default, both the Show the Clock and Hide Inactive Icons check boxes are selected. To remove the time from the Notification area, click the Show the Clock check box to remove the check mark. To display all of the Notification icons, even when the processes they represent are inactive, click the Hide Inactive Icons check box to remove the check mark. Note that when the Hide Inactive Icons setting is active, Windows adds a Show Hidden Icons button that you can click to temporarily display all of the Notification icons.

In addition to changing these two settings for the Notification area, you can change the circumstances under which particular notification icons are displayed in the Notification area. To do this, click the Customize button near the bottom of the Taskbar to open the Customize Notifications dialog box.

The Customize Notifications dialog box contains a list box that is divided into Current Items and Past Items sections. You can change the display status for any icon listed in either section. To do this, click the icon and then click the drop-down button that appears next to the current status (Hide when Inactive is the default setting for all of the icons). To always have the icon displayed in the Notification area, click Always Show in this pop-up menu. To never have the icon appear in this area, click Always Hide instead.

Customizing the Start menu

To customize the appearance of the Start menu, you need to select the Start Menu tab in the taskbar and Start Menu Properties dialog box (note that if you right-click the Start button and then click Properties, the Start Menu tab is automatically the one selected when the Taskbar and Start Menu Properties dialog box opens).

This tab gives you a choice between the Start menu as it now appears in two columns and the old single-column method used in previous versions of Windows. To switch to this single-column view, click the Classic Start Menu radio button. Should you later decide to switch back to the new two-column arrangement, you can do so by clicking the Start Menu radio button.

Both radio buttons are accompanied by Customize buttons that open dialog boxes in which you can change what icons appear on the Start menu. The following figure shows the Customize Start Menu dialog box that appears when you click the Customize button associated with the Start Menu radio button that controls the default two-column Start-menu arrangement.

This dialog box has two tabs: General and Advanced. You use the settings on the General tab to control the size of the icons in the Start menu and the number of program icons displayed in the left column (between the More Programs button at the bottom and the Internet and E-Mail buttons at the top).

If you want to remove the Internet and E-Mail buttons from the Start menu, you're able do so by clicking the Internet and/or E-Mail check boxes to remove those check marks. If you've installed a

Web browser in addition to Internet Explorer (such as Netscape Navigator) or e-mail programs in addition to Outlook Express (such as Outlook or Hotmail), you can select these programs to launch when you click the Internet or E-Mail button on the Start menu. Just click the Internet or E-Mail drop-down button, and select the new Web browser or e-mail program in the pop-up menu.

The options on the Advanced tab of the Customize Start menu enable you to modify which items are displayed in the right column of the Start menu. It also enables you to control whether clicking the buttons of fixed items, such as the My Documents or My Network Places, opens an associated window or a menu from which you can select and open particular components.

For example, currently when you click the Control Panel button on the right side of the Start menu, Windows opens the Control Panel window with links to categories of Control Panels because the Display As a Link setting is in effect. If you change this setting to Display As a Menu, Windows instead displays a menu of all the individual Control Panel options (Accessibility through User Accounts) when you click Control Panel in the Start menu.

To add new icons to the right column of the Start menu, click those check boxes in the Show Menu Items on the Start Menu list box. To change the way fixed icons, such as Control Panel, My Documents, My Computer, and the like, are displayed, click one of the following radio buttons:

- ✔ **Display As a Link:** This radio button is the default setting for all fixed items. It causes Windows to open a folder window showing the item folders and files.

- ✔ **Display As a Menu:** Select this radio button when you want Windows to display the item folders and files as menu items on a continuation menu that you can select and open from the Start menu.

- ✔ **Don't Display This Item:** Select this radio button to remove the display of the fixed item, such as My Network Places.

To display recently opened documents on the Start menu, click the List Most Recently Opened Documents check box at the bottom of the Advanced tab. That way, you can open the document and, at the same time, launch the program by clicking the filename in the Start menu.

Switching between programs

The Windows XP taskbar makes switching between programs as easy as clicking the button representing the program window. All you have to do to activate a program and bring the window to the top of your screen display is click the program button on the taskbar.

Windows old-timers can still use the Alt+Tab shortcut keys, first introduced in Windows 3.0, to switch among all open windows. In Windows XP, however, when you press Alt+Tab, a dialog box appears, with icons for each program window and a description of the icon. When you release the Alt and Tab keys, Windows activates the window for whatever program icon is selected (indicated by the blue box surrounding the icon).

You can switch to another program that you have open any time you need to check something in that program or need to get some work done. You also need to switch to a program so that you can close the window (and thereby shut it down) when you no longer need those services but do need the computer memory that the program is hogging.

Hold down the Alt key as you press the Tab key to open a dialog box that enables you to cycle through icons for all the open windows on the desktop. After you select the icon for the window you want to bring up front (indicated by a blue box around the icon), just release the Alt and Tab keys.

Arranging windows on the desktop

Normally when you open multiple windows on the desktop, they overlap one another, with the most recently opened window fully displayed on top. As you open more windows, it can become increasingly difficult to arrange the windows so that the information you need is displayed on-screen (this is especially true when copying or moving files and folders between open windows).

To help you organize the windows you have open, Windows offers several arrangement options. To rearrange the open windows with one of these options, you need to right-click the Windows taskbar (at a place that isn't occupied by a window button) and then click one of the following options:

- ✔ **Cascade Windows** to overlap the open windows so that the title bars are all displayed one above the other in a cascade.

- ✔ **Tile Windows Horizontally** to place the windows one on top of the other.

- ✔ **Tile Windows Vertically** to place the windows side by side.

- ✔ **Minimize All Windows** to reduce all the open windows to buttons on the Windows taskbar.

- ✔ **Show the Desktop** to reduce all the windows open on the desktop to minimized buttons on the Windows taskbar.

Note that when you tile more than three windows, the windows are arranged both above and to the side of each other (with four windows, the screen appears divided into quadrants), so that you really can't tell whether you selected the Tile Windows Horizontally or the Tile Windows Vertically option. To remove a tiled arrangement, right-click the taskbar once more and this time click the Undo Tile option (added to the shortcut menu whenever you select the Tile Windows Horizontally or the Tile Windows Vertically option).

Using Task Manager

Windows Task Manager keeps tabs on your system and how it's running. You can use Task Manager to get an overview of what programs and processes are running on your computer. You can also use it to switch to programs and to end programs that have stopped responding (in other words have frozen up on you).

To open Windows Task Manager, right-click the taskbar at a place where there are no buttons and then click Task Manager on the shortcut menu. The following figure shows you Windows Task Manager running five different programs.

To switch to another program from Windows Task Manager, click the program in the list box on the Applications tab and then click the Switch To button. Windows will then minimize Task Manager and display the program window on the desktop.

To end a program that has frozen up on you, click the program in the list box on the Applications tab and then click the End Task button. Note that you will probably get an alert dialog box indicating that the program has stopped responding. Click the End button in this dialog box (as many times as you have to) to get Windows to kill the program.

When you click a program in the list on the Applications tab, the status bar of Windows Task Manager shows you statistics on the number of processes running under the program, the percentage of the CPU (Central Processing Unit, the big chip at the heart of the computer), and the memory usage of the program. If you like to look at schematics, click the Performance tab in this window to see a dynamic charting of the total CPU and memory usage on your computer (and to learn really useful stuff like the number of handles, threads, and processes that are being run).

Creating custom toolbars

You can add your own custom toolbars to the Windows taskbar from the folders that you keep on your computer. When you create a custom toolbar from an existing folder, Windows creates buttons for each of the shortcuts and icons that the folder contains.

To create a custom toolbar from a folder, follow these steps:

1. Right-click the taskbar (without clicking any of the buttons or icons it contains) and then choose the Toolbars⇨New Toolbar command on the shortcut menu that appears.

   Windows opens the New Toolbar dialog box, where you enter the pathname of the folder to be used in creating the new toolbar.

2. Select the folder whose contents are to be used in creating the new toolbar by opening the folder in the New Toolbar list box or by typing the directory path in the Folder text box at the bottom.

3. Click the OK button to close the New Toolbar dialog box.

   As soon as you close the New Toolbar dialog box, Windows adds the new toolbar, indicated by a button with the folder's name. When you click this folder button, Windows displays a pop-up menu showing all the subfolders and documents that it contains.

4. (Optional) To remove the new custom toolbar from the taskbar and place it in a separate toolbar window on the desktop or to dock it at the top, left, or right edge of the screen, unlock the taskbar (by right-clicking the bar and then clicking Lock the Taskbar on the shortcut menu) and then drag the toolbar sizing handle to the desired place on the desktop.

5. (Optional) To switch from small to large icons, right-click the toolbar name or the sizing handle (the dotted vertical line at the start) and then click View⇨Large Icons on the shortcut menu. Note that switching to large icons doubles the height of the Windows taskbar.

6. (Optional) To remove the toolbar name, right-click the name of the toolbar and click Show Title on the shortcut menu to remove the check mark.

7. (Optional) To remove the name of the buttons from the toolbar, right-click the toolbar name or the sizing handle (the dotted vertical line at the start) and then click Show Text on the shortcut menu to remove the check mark.

Once you create a custom toolbar for a folder, you can open that folder window on the desktop by right-clicking the toolbar name or the sizing handle and then clicking Open Folder on the shortcut menu.

All custom toolbars that you create last only through your current work session. In other words, whenever you close a custom toolbar or restart your computer, the toolbar is automatically erased, and you must re-create it by using the steps just outlined if you want access to those buttons.

Using Windows Automatic Update

The Windows Update feature notifies you of the latest updates and bug fixes for the Windows XP operating system directly from the Microsoft Web site. To launch the Windows Update, you click the Start menu, point at the All Programs button, and then click Windows Update in the Programs menu.

As soon as you click select Windows Update on this menu, Windows gets you online and connects you to the Windows Update Web page on the Microsoft Web site, shown in the following figure.

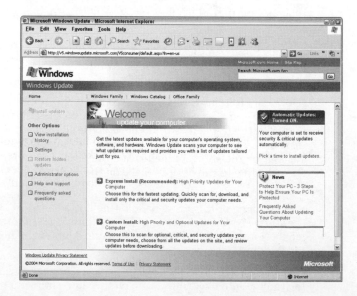

To have your computer checked out to see whether you're in need of some updated Windows components, follow these steps:

1. On the Microsoft Windows Update Web page, click the <u>Express Install (Recommended)</u> hyperlink.

   When you click this hyperlink, the Windows checks your system for critical and security updates. After checking your system, the number of updates appears in the list of High Priority Updates in the pane on the left side of the window.

2. To have the Update Wizard install particular updates in one or more of the various categories, click the check boxes in front of each update name and description.

3. After you have all the updates that you want selected, click the <u>Review and Install Updates</u> hyperlink in the pane on the left side of the window.

4. Click the Start Download button on the Download Checklist page.

   A license agreement dialog box then appears. Choose the Yes button to sell your soul to the devil (just kidding) and start the download.

   After you click the assent to the license agreement, the Microsoft Windows Update page downloads and installs the updated files for the component(s) you selected. When the download and installation are complete, the message <u>Download and Installation Successful</u> appears on the Windows Update Web page.

5. Click the Close box in the upper-right corner of the Microsoft Windows Update Web page to close this browser window.

Just in case you're the type who would never think to use the Windows Update command on the Start menu, Windows XP prompts you to turn on the AutoUpdate feature when you first install Service Pack 2 on your computer. If you click the Help Protect My PC by Turning On Automatic Updates Now option button, the system then automatically checks the Windows Update Web site when you go online, searching for critical and security updates, which it then automatically downloads and installs on your computer.

To modify how often Windows checks for and installs updates, specify that updates be automatically downloaded but not installed or automatically notify you of updates but neither download nor install them, or even turn off the AutoUpdate features (definitely not recommended in this day and age of constant virus and worm attacks), follow these steps:

1. Click the Start button and then click Control Panel.

2. If the Classic View is not shown, click the Switch to Classic View button at the top of the Control Panel navigation pane on the left side of this window.

3. Double-click the System icon to open the Systems Properties dialog box.

4. Click the Automatic Updates tab and then click the option button for the setting change you want to make.

   • Click drop-down buttons under the Automatic option button to change the day and time when Windows checks for, downloads, and installs critical and security updates.

   • Click the Download Updates for Me but Let Me Choose When to Install Them option button to have Windows automatically check for and download critical and security updates and then display an Install Reminder icon in the Notification area of the taskbar that prompts you to install them.

   • Click the Notify Me but Don't Automatically Download or Install Them option button to have Windows automatically check for critical and security updates and then display an Install Reminder icon in the Notification area of the taskbar that prompts you to both download and install them.

   • Click Turn Off Automatic Updates option button to disable this feature entirely.

5. Click OK or press Enter to close the System Properties dialog box.

Part II

Windows and the Web

So what, you may ask, does Windows XP have to do with the World Wide Web? Well, for starters, Windows XP comes with Internet Explorer 6, the latest version of the Microsoft Web browser that makes all your Web browsing easy as can be. Windows also includes version 6 of Outlook Express, the companion e-mail program, equipped with Windows Messenger so that you can do instant messenging/chats with all your friends.

In this part . . .

Adding Web Favorites

You keep bookmarks for all your often-used computer drives and folders and often-visited Web pages in the Favorites folder. The bookmarks that you store in the Favorites folder can point to drives and folders on your computer or network, as well as to Web pages on the Internet.

Most often, however, you'll use the Favorites feature to mark preferred Web pages for easy revisiting. You can access your Favorite bookmarks from the My Documents, Windows Explorer, and My Computer folders windows (in other words, you don't have to be in the Internet Explorer Web browser to use them).

When you first start adding to the Favorites folder, you'll find that it already contains certain folders. The Favorites folder contains a Links and a Mobile Favorites folder (if you connect a handheld device to the computer). In addition, the Favorites folder may contain a folder with your computer manufacturer's favorite Web sites (called something like "XYZ" Corporation Recommended Sites) and a folder called Imported Bookmarks, if you imported bookmarks from the address book created with another Web browser e-mail program into Outlook Express.

To add a bookmark in the Favorites folder for a drive or folder on your computer (or network) or to a Web page on the Internet, follow these steps:

1. Open Internet Explorer 6 and visit the Web page, or open the My Documents, Windows Explorer, or My Computer window and then select the drive and open the folder for which you want to add a bookmark in your Favorites folder. *See* "Navigating the Web" in this part for details on how to open a Web page.

    When adding bookmarks for computer drives or folders, be sure to open the drive or folder and verify that the drive or folder name appears at the end of the path name on the Address Bar. When adding bookmarks for Web pages in Internet Explorer, display the Web page in the browser (the URL appears on the Address Bar).

2. Click Favorites⇨Add to Favorites to open the Add Favorite dialog box.

    If the Favorites Explorer Bar is open, you can also do this by clicking the Add button at the top of this bar (if this Explorer Bar is not visible, you can click the Favorites button — the one with the star — on the Explorer toolbar to open it). The Add Favorite dialog box contains a Name text box with the name of the drive or folder or the title of the Web page that you're adding to the Favorites folder.

3. (Optional) If you want a different bookmark description to appear on the Favorites menu, edit the name that currently appears in the Name text box.

4. (Optional) To add the bookmark in a subfolder of the Favorites folder, click the Create In > button to expand the Add to Favorites dialog box and then click the subfolder icon. To add the bookmark to a new folder, select the icon of the folder in which the new folder is to be inserted and then click the New Folder button in the expanded Add Favorite dialog box, which you see in the following figure. Then enter the folder name in the Create New Folder dialog box and click OK.

5. Click OK to close the Add Favorite dialog box and to add the bookmark to the drive, folder, or Web page to the Favorites menu or folders windows, such as My Documents and My Computer and, of course, Internet Explorer 6.

If you want to add a bookmark to the current Web page to your Favorites folder in Internet Explorer, you can do so simply by dragging the Web page icon (that appears before the page URL in the Address Bar) to the Favorites button on the Standard Buttons toolbar (this button is automatically added to this toolbar in other windows, such as My Documents or My Computer). If you later decide that you want the bookmark to appear in a subfolder of the Favorites folder, you can then move it to the desired subfolder; *see* "Organizing Favorites" a bit later in this part for details.

If the Favorites Explorer Bar is open in the browsing window at the time you want to add the page, you can drag the Web page icon and drop it into this part of the window. To place the new favorite in a particular folder that's displayed in the Favorites Explorer Bar, drag the Web page icon to that folder icon, and drop it in. To have the new Favorite appear at a particular place in the Explorer Bar list, drag the Web page icon to that position in the list (indicated by the appearance of a heavy, horizontal I-beam in the list) before dropping it in place.

You can also add the current page as a Favorite and, simultaneously, place it in the correct folder by right-clicking somewhere on the Web page and then choosing Add to Favorites on the shortcut menu. Doing this opens the Add Favorite dialog box, which you can use as I describe in the previous steps.

Opening Favorites

After you add a computer drive, folder, or Internet Web page to your Favorites folder (or one of the subfolders), you can open the item simply by selecting the bookmark, either from the Favorites pull-down menu or from the Favorites Explorer Bar.

To select a bookmark from the Favorites pull-down menu in folder windows (such as My Computer or Windows Explorer) or in the Internet Explorer 6 window, choose Favorites on the menu bar and then select the name of the bookmark on the Favorites menu. If the bookmark is located in a subfolder of the Favorites, you need to drill down to the subfolder icon to open the submenu, where you can click the desired bookmark.

To select a bookmark from the Favorites Explorer Bar, open the Explorer Bar by choosing View➪Explorer Bar➪Favorites on the window menu bar or by pressing Ctrl+I (in Internet Explorer 6, just click the Favorites button on the Standard Buttons toolbar). Now click the bookmark hyperlink. If the bookmark is located in a subfolder of Favorites, click the folder icon to expand the list and display the bookmarks; then click the hyperlink for the bookmark to the drive, folder, or Web page that you want to open.

 When you click a bookmark to a Web page in a folders window, such as My Documents or My Computer, Windows XP connects you to the Internet and automatically converts that window into the Internet Explorer Web browser.

Offline Favorites

When you add a bookmark to a Web site, you can also mark the Web pages so that they're available for offline viewing (that is, when your computer is *not* connected to the Internet). In order to make all or part of the Web site pages available for offline viewing, Windows *caches* the Web page content by downloading it and saving it in a special location on your computer hard drive. As part of this process, Windows also sets up a schedule (which you can customize) for synchronizing the offline pages cached on your computer with the pages on the Internet so that the offline pages are kept up to date.

To mark a Web site for offline viewing, follow these steps:

1. Visit the Web site whose pages you want to view offline in Internet Explorer 6 (*see* "Navigating the Web" later in this part for details).

2. Choose Favorites⇨Add to Favorites to open the Add Favorite dialog box.

3. Click the Make Available Offline check box to put a check mark in it.

4. (Optional) To customize how much of the site is made available for offline viewing (that is, cached on your computer) and/or to change the schedule used in synchronizing new Web content, choose the Customize button to open the Offline Favorite wizard and then follow the directions for changing how much of the site is downloaded and how often the contents are synchronized.

   To have more than just the home page of the site cached on your computer, select the Yes radio button in the second dialog box of the Offline Favorite wizard and then select the number of levels that you want pages downloaded in the Download Pages text box.

   By default, Windows synchronizes only the cached pages with the ones online when you choose Tools⇨Synchronize on the menu bar. To set up your own automated schedule in the third dialog box, select the radio button marked I Would Like to Create a New Schedule; then choose Next, and specify the daily interval and time for synchronization in the appropriate text boxes. If you want Windows to automatically connect your computer to the Internet when this time interval occurs, select the radio button called If My Computer Is Not Connected When the Scheduled Synchronization Begins, Automatically Connect for Me.

   To use an existing daily, weekly, or monthly schedule, choose the radio button called Using This Existing Schedule (if this button is available for this Web site) in the third dialog box; then choose the appropriate interval in the drop-down list box immediately below this button.

   If the Web site that you're marking for offline viewing requires you to give a login ID and password in order to gain entrance, use Next to go to the last dialog box of the Offline Favorite Wizard, and select the radio button that says Yes, My User Name and Password Are. Then enter your user name and password in the appropriate text boxes before you click the Finish button.

   5. (Optional) To add the bookmark to the Web page in a subfolder of the Favorites folder, click the Create In > button to
   expand the Add to Favorites dialog box. Then click the subfolder icon. To add the bookmark to a new folder, select the
   icon of the folder in which you want the new folder inserted
   and then click the New Folder button in the expanded Add
   Favorite dialog box. Next, enter the folder name in the Create
   New Folder dialog box, and click OK.

   6. Click OK to close the Add Favorite dialog box: This action adds
   the bookmark to the Web page to the Favorites menu of all
   folders and browsing windows (such as My Documents, My
   Computer, and Internet Explorer 6) and completes the subscription to the Web page.

After clicking OK, the Synchronizing dialog box appears, showing
the progress of the downloading of the page(s) that you marked for
offline viewing. When Windows completes downloading the
page(s), the message Synchronization Complete appears in
the dialog box right before Windows closes it.

If, after adding just a plain old bookmark to a Web page, you decide
that you want to make it available for offline viewing, you can still
do so. Just right-click the bookmark on the Favorites pull-down
menu or Explorer Bar and choose the Make Available Offline command on the shortcut menu. This action opens the Offline Favorite
Wizard, where you can customize the synchronization settings (as I
describe in the preceding Step 4). To accept the settings, choose
Next until you reach the last dialog box in the wizard, where you
click the Finish button.

To view a favorite Web page that's been made available offline,
select File⇨Work Offline from the Internet Explorer menu bar and
then open the cached page by choosing it from the Favorites pull-
down menu or Explorer Bar.

See also "Working offline" later in this part for more on viewing
cached pages when you're not connected to the Internet. and
"Synchronizing offline favorites" for information on synchronizing
the cached Web content.

Organizing Favorites

Many times, you'll find yourself going along adding bunches of bookmarks to your preferred Web pages without ever bothering to create
them in particular subfolders. Then, to your dismay, you'll find yourself confronted with a seemingly endless list of unrelated bookmarks
every time you open the Favorites submenu or Explorer Bar.

Fortunately, Windows makes it easy to reorganize even the most
chaotic of bookmark lists in just a few easy steps:

1. Open a folder window, such as My Documents, Windows Explorer, or My Computer, or Internet Explorer 6 and then choose Favorites➪Organize Favorites to open the Organize Favorites dialog box.

The list box of the Organize Favorites dialog box shows all the subfolders, followed by all the bookmarks in the Favorites folder.

2. To move bookmarks into one of the subfolders of Favorites, select those icons and then click the Move to Folder button to open the Browse for Folder dialog box. Click the destination folder in the Browse for Folder dialog box and then click OK.

Use the following options in the Organize Favorites dialog box to create new folders to hold your bookmarks, to rename bookmarks, or even to get rid of unwanted bookmarks:

✔ To create a new folder, click the Create Folder icon to add a new folder icon; then type a new name for the folder, and press Enter.

✔ To rename a link to a favorite drive, folder, or Web page, click the icon to select it, click the Rename button, edit the item name, and then press Enter.

✔ To delete a link to a favorite drive, folder, or Web page, click the icon and then click the Delete button. Click Yes in the Confirm File Delete dialog box when it asks whether you're sure that you want to send that particular favorite to the Recycle Bin.

 Don't delete or rename the Links folder in the Organize Favorites dialog box. Internet Explorer 6 needs the Links folder so that it knows what buttons to display on the Links bar.

 You can also use the drag-and-drop method to do some quick reordering of the bookmarks in the Organize Favorites dialog box. Just drag the bookmark to the desired folder in the list box, and release the mouse button.

Note that you can also use drag-and-drop in the Favorites Explorer Bar to change the order of the bookmarks within a particular folder or to move bookmarks to new folders. Just open the Favorites Explorer bar in a folder window or Internet Explorer (Ctrl+I or View⇨Explorer Bar⇨Favorites) and then use one of these techniques:

✔ To open one of the folders on the Explorer Bar to display the folder contents, click the folder icon. Internet Explorer then displays a series of icons for each of the subfolders and bookmarks it contains. To close a folder to hide the contents, click the folder icon again.

✔ To move a bookmark to a new position in the folder, drag that icon up or down until you reach the desired position. As you drag, you see where the item will be inserted by the appearance of a heavy, horizontal I-beam between the bookmarks. You also see where you *cannot* move the icon because of the display of the international no-no symbol.

✔ To move a bookmark icon to a different (existing) folder, drag the bookmark icon to the folder icon. When the folder icon is highlighted, you can drop the favorite icon into it.

Synchronizing offline Favorites

From time to time, you may want Internet Explorer to synchronize the content of some or all the offline favorite Web pages cached on your computer hard drive with that of their online counterparts on the Internet. To synchronize your offline favorites, follow these steps:

1. Launch Internet Explorer and then choose Tools⇨Synchronize on the Explorer menu bar to open the Items to Synchronize dialog box.

The Items to Synchronize dialog box lists all the Web pages that you've marked for offline viewing, along with all the Desktop items that you've added to your desktop. *See* "Saving Desktop items" later in this part for information on this type of cached Web content.

2. In the list box of the Items to Synchronize dialog box, make sure that all the pages you want checked for new content have check marks in the check boxes. Remove the check marks from all Web pages and Desktop items that you don't want synchronized.

3. Click the Synchronize button at the bottom of the dialog box to close the Items to Synchronize dialog box and open the Synchronizing dialog box.

The Synchronizing dialog box shows you the downloading progress of new Web content for the offline Web pages you selected in the Items to Synchronize dialog box. When Windows finishes downloading the new content for the pages in question, this Synchronizing dialog box automatically disappears.

If you feel the need, you can stop the downloading of new content for the currently selected page by clicking the Stop button. If you decide that you don't want a page somewhere down in the list to be synchronized after all, click that name and then click the Skip button to remove it.

 You can control when offline Web content is synchronized by clicking the Setup button at the bottom of the Items to Synchronize dialog box. This action opens the Synchronization Settings dialog box, with the following three tabs:

✓ **Logon/Logoff tab:** Use the check box settings on this tab to indicate which page content to update each time you connect to or disconnect from the Internet.

✓ **On Idle tab:** Use these check-box settings to indicate what content to update when your computer is connected to the Internet but is also idle.

✓ **Scheduled tab:** Use these tab buttons to modify the time and the interval when pages marked for offline viewing are automatically updated (assuming that you're connected to the Internet at that time).

Browsing with Internet Explorer

Windows XP includes Internet Explorer 6, which enables you to browse Web pages anywhere on the Internet. This most recent version of the Microsoft Web browser is equipped with all the latest and greatest features for helping you find, visit, and retrieve any online information that might interest you.

Two basic steps are involved in browsing Web pages with the Internet Explorer 6 browser:

- Connecting to the Internet

- Going to the Web page

You can also browse Web pages from a folder window, such as My Documents and My Computer. When you select a Web page in one of these windows (either by typing the URL in the Address Bar or selecting a bookmarked Web page on the Favorites menu or Explorer Bar), Windows converts the erstwhile My Documents or My Computer window into a bona fide Internet Explorer window).

Connecting to the Internet

You connect to the Internet either with a dial-up modem or a cable or DSL modem connection (both of which use a modem directly connected to your computer) or with a connection to a LAN that's connected to the Internet through some sort of high-speed telephone line, such as a T1 or T3.

When you connect to the Internet via a dial-up connection (as you normally do at home), your modem must call up an Internet service provider (ISP), such as AT&T WorldNet, or a bulletin-board service, such as America Online (AOL), whose high-speed telephone lines and fancy switching equipment provide you (for a fee) with access to the Internet and all the online services.

When you connect to the Internet via a cable or DSL modem or a LAN (as you normally would in a large corporation or at a university), you don't have to do anything special to get connected to the Internet: You have Internet access any time you turn on your computer and launch Internet Explorer.

Launching Internet Explorer

To launch Internet Explorer, click the Start button on the Windows taskbar and then click the Internet option at the very top of the Start menu. (If the Internet Explorer is not listed as the Internet option, point to All Programs and then click Internet Explorer on the continuation menu.) You can also simply click the Launch Internet Explorer Browser icon (the one with the blue *e*) in the Quick Launch toolbar that appears on the Windows taskbar.

Whenever you launch Internet Explorer 6, it automatically attempts to go to the Web page address that is listed as the home page on the General tab of the Internet Options dialog box (Tools⇨Internet Options). If your computer is configured to use a dial-up connection,

Windows also automatically begins the process of connecting to your ISP, based on your current dial-up settings.

If Windows can't connect to the home page (either because of heavy traffic on the Web site or technical difficulties with the site ISP or your ISP — so much can go wrong!), it displays an alert box with an obscure error message, whereupon Internet Explorer 6 displays a Web page called about:NavigationCanceled in the Address bar.

Navigating the Web

After the connection is made and the home page appears in the browsing window, you're free to begin browsing other pages on the World Wide Web by doing any of the following:

✔ Entering the Uniform Resource Locator (URL) of the Web page in the Address Bar and pressing Enter or clicking the Go button

✔ Clicking hyperlinks on the currently displayed Web page that take you to other Web pages, either on the same Web site or on another Web site

✔ Selecting a bookmarked Web page that appears on the Favorites menu or Explorer Bar, or one that you've recently visited on the History Explorer Bar (*see* "Adding Web Favorites" earlier in this part for details on how to add Web pages to the Favorites menu)

✔ Using the MSN Web search engine to display hyperlinks for the home pages of Web sites that might possibly fit some search criteria, such as "IRA investments" or, better yet, "Hawaiian vacations" (*see* "Searching the Web" later in this part for details on searching)

After you start exploring different Web pages via URLs or hyperlinks as I describe previously, you can start clicking the Back button on the Standard Buttons toolbar to return to any of the previously viewed pages. Each time you click Back (or press Alt+←), Internet Explorer goes back to the very last page you viewed. If you've visited several pages during the same browsing session, you can jump to a particular page that you viewed by clicking the drop-down button that appears to the immediate right of the Back button and then selecting the page name from the drop-down list. Note that you can also go back to a previous page or forward to the once current page by right-clicking the Web page and then selecting Back or Forward on the page's shortcut menu.

After using the Back button to revisit one or more previously viewed pages, the Forward button (right next door) becomes active. Click the Forward button (or press Alt+→) to step forward through each of the pages that you've viewed with the Back button, or select a page to jump to in the Forward button drop-down list.

If you come upon a page that doesn't seem to want to load, for some reason (including a broken hyperlink or too much Web traffic), click the Stop button on the Standard buttons bar to stop the process; then select a new Web site to visit. When revisiting a page, you can make sure that the content currently displayed by Internet Explorer is completely up to date by clicking the Refresh button (to the immediate right of the Stop button on the Standard Buttons toolbar).

Address AutoComplete

Of all the methods for browsing pages on the Web that I mention in the list in the preceding section, none is quite as bad as having to type URL addresses with the **http://** and the **www** something or other **.com**s in the Address Bar. To help eliminate errors in typing and speed this tedious process, Windows employs a feature called AutoComplete. This nifty feature looks at whatever few characters of the URL address you type in the Address Bar and, based on them, attempts to match them to one of the complete addresses that are stored in the Address Bar drop-down list.

For example, if you click the cursor in the Address Bar and then select all the characters in the current Web address that follow http://www (the standard beginning for most Web addresses) and then replace the last part of the current address with the letter *h*, AutoComplete opens the Address Bar drop-down list, displaying all the Web sites that you've visited whose first letter in the URL (after the standard http://www. stuff) begins with *h*.

To visit any one of the pages listed in the Address Bar drop-down list, click that name in the drop-down list. Internet Explorer then enters the complete URL address of the Web site you clicked in the Address Bar and automatically displays the page.

The AutoComplete feature also works when you browse folders on a local or network disk. To display a list of recently viewed documents on your hard drive, type the letter of your hard drive, followed by a colon, in the Address Bar (**C:**, in most cases); then click the document you want to open in Internet Explorer in the Address Bar drop-down list.

Saving Web graphics

As you're browsing Web pages with Internet Explorer, you may come upon some sites that offer graphic images for downloading. You can save Web graphics on your computer hard drive in one of the following three ways:

✔ As a graphic file for viewing and printing in the My Pictures folder; *see* "My Pictures" in Part I. To do this, right-click the graphic and then click Save Picture As on the image shortcut menu.

✔ As the wallpaper for your desktop (*see* "Display" in Part IV). To do this, right-click the graphic and then click Set as Background on the image shortcut menu.

✔ As a Desktop item that appears on your computer desktop; *see* "Saving Desktop Items" later in this part. To do this, right-click the graphic and then choose Set as Desktop Item on the image shortcut menu.

 Note that if you save a Web graphic as the wallpaper for your desktop, you have a choice between tiling the image (that is, duplicating it across the entire desktop), centering it in the middle of the desktop, or stretching it so that it fills the entire desktop (which most often results in a severely distorted image).

Saving Web pages

Occasionally, you may want to save an entire Web page on your computer (text, hyperlinks, graphics, and all). To save the Web page that currently appears in Internet Explorer, choose File⊅Save As to open the Save Web Page dialog box. Select the folder in which you want the page saved and then click the Save button.

After saving a Web page on your hard drive, you can open it in Internet Explorer and view the contents even when you're not connected to the Internet. If your motive for saving the Web page, however, is to be able to view the content when you're not connected to the Internet, you're better off saving the page as a Favorite marked for offline viewing. That way, you can decide whether you want to view other pages linked to the one you're saving, and you can have Internet Explorer check the site for updated content. *See* "Offline Favorites" earlier in this part for details.

You can also e-mail a Web page or a link to the page to a colleague or friend. To send the current Web page in a new e-mail message, click File⇨Send⇨Page by E-mail on the Explorer menu bar and then fill out the new e-mail; *see* "Sending and Receiving E-Mail" later in this part for details). To send a link to the page instead, click File⇨Send⇨Link by E-Mail. To create a desktop shortcut to the Web page, click File⇨Send⇨Shortcut to Desktop.

Saving Desktop items

Desktop items (also known as Web items) are smaller, special versions of Web pages that reside right on your computer desktop. As with Favorite Web pages that you mark for offline viewing (*see* "Offline Favorites" earlier in this part for details), you view Desktop items when you aren't connected to the Internet. As with offline Favorites, you can also synchronize the Desktop items on your computer desktop with the ones on the Internet so that all the content is totally up to date — a very important feature when you're dealing with volatile Web items, such as the MSNBC Weather Map and the Microsoft Investor stock ticker!

The best place to get Desktop items is the Microsoft Desktop Gallery page. The Internet address is

`www.microsoft.com/windows/ie/gallery/`

This Web page offers several favorite Desktop items, such as the Microsoft Investor stock ticker, which you can use to track the ups and downs of your favorite stocks (especially the ones in which you've invested), and the Weather Map from MSNBC, which gives you an update on the current weather in any part of the United States.

To download Desktop items, such as these from the Desktop Gallery, browse to the Web page and then click the item's Add to Active Desktop button. An alert box appears asking if you want to add an Active Desktop item to your desktop. After you click the Yes button, the Add Item to Active Desktop dialog box appears; click the OK button to begin downloading the item.

After you add a Desktop item, you can move the graphic around the desktop: Simply position the mouse pointer on the graphic until the title bar appears at the top and then drag the item to the new position by the title bar. You can also resize some desktop items. To do this, position the mouse pointer on the lower-right corner of the item, and drag the mouse diagonally. To fix all your desktop items in their current positions on the desktop, right-click the desktop, then point to Arrange Icons By, and click Lock Web Items on Desktop at the bottom of the continuation menu that appears.

You can turn off the display of any individual Desktop item that you add to the desktop by clicking the close button that appears in the upper-right corner of the title bar (which appears when you hover the mouse over the item), or you can do it from the Display Properties dialog box (*see* "Appearance and Themes" in Part IV for details).

Printing Web pages

Many times when browsing Web pages in Internet Explorer 6, you want to print the pages you visit. Internet Explorer 6 not only makes it easy to print the Web pages you go to see, but also gives you the ability to preview the printout before you commit your printer.

To preview the current Web page, choose File⇨Print Preview on the Internet Explorer menu bar. Doing this opens a full-screen Print Preview window similar to the one shown in the following figure. The Print Preview toolbar at the top of this window contains some important buttons for checking out how many paper pages are required to print all the information on the Web page and what information is to be printed on which paper page:

- ✔ To advance back and forth through the preview a page at a time, click the Next Page or Previous Page button (or press Alt+→ or Alt+←, respectively).

- ✔ To advance to the first page of the preview, click the First Page button (or press Alt+Home). To advance to the last page of the preview, click the Last Page button (or press Alt+End).

- ✔ To zoom out to see more of the previewed page in the Print Preview window, click the Zoom Out button (or press Alt+minus sign). To zoom in on the page to see more detail, click the Zoom In button (or press Alt+plus sign).

- ✔ To change the page setup settings (including such things as the paper size, margins, and orientation of the printing), click the Page Setup button (or press Alt+U) to open the Page Setup dialog box.

✔ To go ahead and print the page(s) as it appears in the Print Preview window, click the Print button (or press Alt+P) to open the Print dialog box. To close the Print Preview window without printing the page, click the Close button (or press Alt+C).

Next Page

Previous Page | Last Page

First Page | Zoom Out

Page Setup | Zoom In

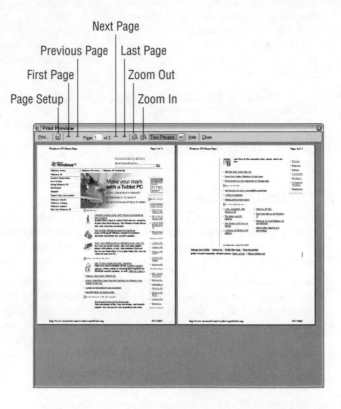

If you choose not to print from the Print Preview screen, or you're sure that you don't need to use Print Preview to get the information you want, you can print the Web page currently displayed in Internet Explorer by choosing File⇨Print to open the Print dialog box. In this dialog box, you can specify such options as the printer name, pages to print, and number of copies before you click the Print button to send the pages to the printer.

Working offline

With the advent of Web items and Web page subscriptions comes the appearance of so-called *offline* browsing (as opposed to *online* browsing, which indicates being connected to the Internet). Because you can set up the Favorites that you mark for offline viewing (*see* "Offline Favorites" earlier in this part) so that their updated content is automatically downloaded to your hard drive (normally during the wee hours, when you're safely tucked in your beddy-bye and only wild-eyed nerds are surfing the Net), you can use offline browsing to view the updated Web contents with Internet Explorer 6 at your leisure.

Offline browsing is especially beneficial when you're using a laptop computer and can't get connected to the Internet (as when in transit on a bus, train, or plane). It can also come in handy when you rely on a relatively slow dial-up connection (as with 28.8 or 33.3 Kbps modems) to the Internet, enabling you to download Web content during nonpeak hours and browse it with maximum efficiency during the peak surfing hours (thereby totally avoiding the "World Wide Wait").

To turn offline browsing on and off, choose File➪Work Offline from the Internet Explorer pull-down menus. Note that after you put the browsing window in offline mode, it remains in this work mode until you restart your computer. In other words, if you shut down the browsing window and then launch it again during the same work session, it opens in offline mode. If you decide that you want to do some serious online surfing, you need to start by choosing the File➪Work Offline command to turn off the offline mode.

When offline mode is on (indicated by a check mark in front of the Work Offline command on the File menu), Windows will not automatically attempt to connect to the Internet, and you can browse only pages stored locally on your computer, such as those that have been downloaded into the cache on your computer hard drive. Also known as the Temporary Internet Files, the cache contains all Web pages and their components that are downloaded when you subscribe to Web sites or channels.

 When you browse a Web site offline from a local drive, you have none of the wait often associated with browsing online when connected to the Internet. You may also find, however, that some of the links, especially those to pages on another Web site that you haven't marked as Favorites, aren't available for offline viewing. Internet Explorer lets you know when a link isn't available by adding the international "No" or "Don't" symbol (you know, the circle with a backslash in it) to the hand cursor.

If you persist and click a hyperlink to a page that has not been downloaded with the hand-plus-Don't-symbol cursor, the browsing window displays an alert dialog box, indicating that the Web page you requested is not available offline. To have Internet Explorer connect you to the Internet and go to the requested page, click the Connect button or press Enter. To remain offline and close the alert dialog box, click the Stay Offline button instead.

Most of the time when browsing offline, you do your local Web surfing in one of two ways:

✔ Visit updated Web pages stored in the cache as Favorites marked for offline viewing. You open these pages by selecting them from the Favorite Explorer Bar (opened by clicking the Favorites button) or by choosing them from the Favorites pull-down menu; *see* "Offline Favorites" earlier in this part for details.

✔ Revisit Web pages stored in the cache as part of the History. You open these pages by selecting them from the History Explorer Bar, which you open by pressing Ctrl+H, by clicking the History button on the Explorer toolbar (the one with the arrow curving around backwards), or by clicking View➪Explorer Bar➪History on the Internet Explorer menu bar.

In addition to using these two browsing methods, you can open Web pages that are stored in folders on local disks, such as the hard drive or a CD-ROM in your CD-ROM drive. The easiest way to open these pages is by selecting the drive letter in the Address Bar of Internet Explorer. You can also open a local Web page with the Open dialog box (choose File➪Open or press Ctrl+O).

Browsing with MSN Explorer

In Windows XP, Internet Explorer is not the only Microsoft browser you can use to visit your favorite Web sites. This version of Windows also offers you the opportunity of using MSN Explorer to do the job. Using MSN Explorer to surf the Internet is a little different from using Internet Explorer. For one thing, each time you use MSN Explorer, you must sign in using a Hotmail user ID and password (which, if you don't already have one, you sign up for the first time you open MSN Explorer). For another thing, each time you sign on, MSN Explorer takes you to a version of the MSN.com Web site customized to your locale (as indicated by your local address and ZIP code, which you give as part of the sign-up procedure) so that the opening page displays your local weather and top news stories along with the general topics.

To start MSN Explorer, click the Start button on the taskbar, point at All Programs, and then click MSN Explorer on the All Programs continuation menu. The first time you launch MSN Explorer, an alert dialog box appears, asking you if you would "like to get on the Internet and write e-mail through the Start menu using MSN Explorer." Click the Yes button (you can also click the Don't Show Message Again check box so you're not bothered with this question again before selecting Yes) to close the Use MSN Explorer dialog box.

When you click the Yes button, Windows opens the Welcome to
MSN Explorer window. To sign in and open the MSN.com Web site,
type your password in the Enter Your Password text box and then
click the Sign In button.

Windows opens a customized version of the home page of the
MSN.com Web site. The following figure shows an opening page
customized for my account. This page shows the weather at the
Point Reyes Lighthouse on a Local Weather pop-up menu if you
click the Point Reyes Station button that appears at the very top
of the My Stuff pane on the left, because this is very close to my
home.

MSN Explorer is divided into two main sections: a My Stuff pane on
the left side and the main browsing area on the right. At the top of
the browsing window, you find a toolbar with the following buttons:

- ✔ **Goes Back to Previous Page** to return to a previously viewed
  page.

- ✔ **Goes Forward After Going Back** to return to the page you were
  visiting just before you clicked the Goes Back to Previous Page
  button.

- ✔ **Home** to return to your customized MSN home page.

- ✔ **E-mail** to get your Hotmail messages and to send new e-mail
  using this account (**see** "Retrieving e-mail via Windows
  Messenger" later in this part).

  ✔ **Favorites** to display a list of links to the favorite pages you
    mark in MSN Explorer or to add Web pages that you visit to
    your list of favorites.

  ✔ **Online Contacts** to select an online buddy or add a new buddy
    for doing instant messaging with MSN Messenger Service (*see*
    "Instant messaging" later in this part for details).

  ✔ **People & Chat** to open the People & Chat page, where you can
    locate and join an online chat or locate and join an online com-
    munity with which to communicate.

  ✔ **Money** to open the MoneyCentral page, with links for finding
    out all the latest financial news and for tracking your stocks and
    portfolio.

  ✔ **Shopping** to open the eShop page, where you can locate all
    sorts of online retailers ranging from Apparel & Accessories to
    Toys, Games, and Education.

  ✔ **Music** to open the Music page in the WindowsMedia.com site,
    where you can purchase your favorites tunes or download the
    latest music and videos.

  ✔ **Games** to open Zone.com in the MSN browser, where you can
    play different types of games, including puzzles, trivia, card and
    board, and casino-type games.

Beneath this toolbar, right above the main browsing area, you find
a second toolbar that contains these buttons:

  ✔ **Address Bar:** Enter the URL address of the Web site you want to
    visit in the Address Bar.

  ✔ **Go:** Click the Go button to visit the Web site whose URL
    address is listed in the Address Bar.

  ✔ **Stop:** Click the Stop button to stop loading a Web page that is
    taking a long time to display.

  ✔ **Print:** Click the Print button to print the Web page currently dis-
    played in MSN Explorer.

  ✔ **Refresh:** Click the Refresh button to reload the page and to
    update the content currently displayed in the MSN browsing
    window.

  ✔ **More Choices:** Click this button to display a pop-up menu of
    choices, including New Window, to open a new browsing
    window Find on Page to search for some text in the current Web
    page, and Help to get online help in using MSN Explorer.

When you first start using MSN Explorer, the My Stuff area on the left side contains the following buttons at the top of the bar:

✓ **My Calendar:** Use this button to set up your future appointments and then have the MSN Calendar remind you of them.

✓ **My Stocks:** Use this button to add all your favorite stock symbols to a pop-up list so that you can view the latest selling price simply by clicking the My Stocks button. To add stock symbols to this pop-up list, click the Go to My Stocks hyperlink at the bottom.

✓ **My Groups:** Use this button to list all of the online communities that you join (in wide-ranging areas from Business to Sports and Recreation). To browse and join communities of your choice, click the My Web Sites button and then click the Open My Web Sites hyperlink at the bottom of the pop-up list. To visit the Web pages for a community that you join, click that link in the pop-up list.

✓ **My Horoscope:** Use this button to open the MSN Astrology page, where you can get your personalized horoscope.

✓ **My Photos:** Use this button to create Web pages for your favorite photos, which you can share with everyone on the Web.

✓ **Unnamed button with two triangles pointing to the right:** Use this button to select the Minimize (or Maximize) option to minimize (or maximize) this bar or to select the Personalize My Stuff option to open the Member Center page, where you can view and customize the items in the My Stuff area.

These buttons are followed by a Search the Web text box that you can use to search for new sites (*see* "Searching the Web," which follows) and a collapsed version of Media Player, which you can use to listen to online audio and video that you access with the browser.

To customize the buttons in the My Stuff bar, click the Help & Settings button on the top-right side of the MSN Explorer title bar to display the Member Center page. On this page, click the Personalize My Stuff hyperlink (numbered 8 in the list of things you can customize). Or you can click the button with the two triangles pointing to the right at the bottom of the My Stuff area and then click Personalize My Stuff item on the pop-up menu.

Doing this takes you to a Change My Stuff page that shows the current list of buttons and is followed by a list of the other buttons (from My Files to My Mobile) that you can add. To add a new button to the My Stuff area, click the Add This! button beneath the icon used to represent the area (for example, underneath the football and basketball icon used to represent the My Sports button).

To remove an existing button, click the Remove button to the right of the name at the top of this page. To advance a button by placing it higher in the list in the My Stuff area, click the button that has the triangle pointing up. To demote a button by placing it lower in the list in the My Stuff area, click the button that has the triangle pointing down.

When you're finished browsing with MSN Explorer, you have a choice of closing the browser but not signing off (so that you're still connected to the MSN.com Web site and can receive updates and instant messages) or closing the browser and signing off.

To close the browser but stay signed on, click the Close button (the one with the X) on the far-right side of the MSN Explorer title bar and then click the OK button in the alert dialog box that appears. This dialog box tells you that after closing all MSN Explorer windows, you will still be signed in, and MSN Explorer will continue to run in the background in the Notification area of the taskbar so that you can continue to receive notifications and instant messages. To sign off when you close all MSN Explorer windows, click Sign Out and then click the Close button in the MSN Welcome screen to close all open MSN Explorer windows.

Searching the Web

The World Wide Web holds an enormous wealth of information on almost every subject known to humanity — and it's of absolutely no use if you don't know how to get to it. To help Web surfers such as yourself locate the sites containing the information you need, a number of so-called *search engines* have been designed. Each search engine maintains a slightly different directory of the sites on the World Wide Web (which are mostly maintained and updated by automated programs called by such wonderfully suggestive names as Web crawlers, spiders, and robots!). Internet Explorer 6 and MSN Explorer use the MSN Search engine to find your next new favorite Web sites.

Searching from the Explorer Bar

Internet Explorer 6 makes it easy to search the World Wide Web from the Search Companion Explorer Bar. You can open the Search Companion bar in one of three ways:

✔ Click the Search button on the Standard Buttons toolbar

✔ Press Ctrl+E (which acts as a toggle for both opening and closing the Search Companion bar)

✔ Choose View⇨Explorer Bar⇨Search

The Search Companion bar contains a text box where you enter a description of the type of sites you want to locate. After you've entered the keyword or words (known affectionately as a *search string* in programmers' parlance) to search for in this text box, you begin the search by clicking the Search button.

Internet Explorer conducts a search for Web sites containing the keywords and then displays the first 15 results in the Web Search page of the MSN.com Web site. It also lists links to related sites in the Search Companion bar under the heading "What would you like to do?" Each item in the Search pane also consists of links (which are sequentially numbered) that you can click to visit the site, followed by a description of the site contents and the URL address.

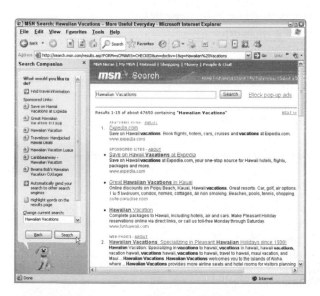

To visit a site in this list, click the hyperlink. To view the next group of 10 to 20 results of the Web search (depending upon your current screen resolution), click the <u>Next</u> hyperlink at the top of the MSN Search page. To redisplay the search results from a Web page that you visit, click the Back button or press Alt+←.

After you're convinced that you've seen the best matches to your search, but you still haven't found the Web site(s) you're looking for, you can conduct another search in the Search Companion Explorer Bar by using slightly different terms.

Autosearching from the Address Bar

In addition to searching from the Search Companion Explorer Bar, Windows enables you to perform searches from the Internet Explorer Address Bar by using a feature referred to as Autosearching. To conduct an Autosearch from the Address Bar, you need to click the Address Bar to select the current entry and then preface the search string with one of the following three terms:

- ✔ Go

- ✔ Find

- ✔ ?

To search for Web sites whose descriptions contain the terms *Thai cuisine,* for example, you could type

```
go Thai cuisine
```

or

```
find Thai cuisine
```

or even

```
? Thai cuisine
```

in the Address Bar. After you enter **go**, **find**, or **?** followed by the search string, press the Enter key to have Windows conduct the search.

When you press Enter, Internet Explorer opens the MSN Search page with the first 10 to 20 matches to your search string (depending upon your screen resolution).

Sending and Receiving E-Mail

Outlook Express 6 is the name of the e-mail software that is installed with Windows XP. You can use this program to compose, send, and read e-mail messages and to subscribe to the newsgroups supported by your Internet service provider, which enables you to read the newsgroup messages as well as respond to them.

Composing and sending messages

To compose and send a new e-mail message in Outlook Express,
follow these steps:

1. Click the Launch Outlook Express button on the Quick Launch
toolbar on the Windows taskbar to start Outlook Express in a
full-screen window, as shown in the following figure.

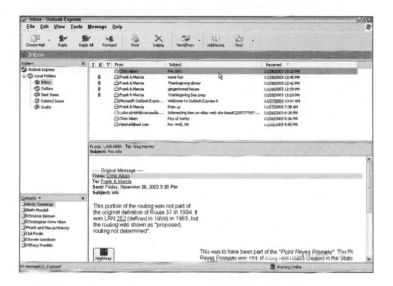

The Outlook Express window contains three panes: Folders,
Contacts (both on the left side), and the larger Outlook
Express pane (on the right side).

2. Click the Create Mail button on the Outlook Express toolbar to
open a New Message dialog box, or choose Message⇨New
Message (or simply press Ctrl+N) to open a New Message
window.

The first thing to do in a new message is to specify the recipient's e-mail address in the To: field (which automatically contains the cursor). You can either type this address in the To:
text box or click the To button to display the Select Recipients
dialog box, in which you can select the recipients from a list of
contacts in your Windows Address Book or from one of the
online directories.

TIP

To send a new message to someone who's already listed in
your Address Book, double-click the person's name in the
Contacts pane of the Outlook Express window. Outlook
Express will then open a New Message window, with the recipient's e-mail address already entered in the To: field.

Alternatively, you can type the recipient's e-mail address in the text box of the To: field or, if the recipient is listed in your Windows Address Book, click the To button to open the Select Recipients dialog box. Click the name of the recipient in the Name list box, then click the To button, and finally click OK.

When composing a new message, you can send copies of it to as many other recipients (within reason) as you want. To send copies of the message to other recipients, type their e-mail addresses in the Cc: field.

3. (Optional) Click somewhere in the Cc: field and then type the e-mail addresses, separated by semicolons (;), in the Cc: field. Alternatively, if the addresses appear in the Windows Address Book, click the Cc button to open the Select Recipients dialog box and then choose the e-mail addresses there (after clicking the names in the Name list box, click the Cc button to add them to the copy list).

After filling in the e-mail addresses of the recipients, you're ready to enter the subject of the message. The descriptive text that you type in the Subject: field of the message appears in the upper pane of the recipients' Inbox when they read the message.

4. Click somewhere in the Subject: field and then enter a brief description of the contents or purpose of the e-mail message.

In Outlook Express, you can change the priority of the e-mail message from normal to high or low. When you make a message either high or low priority, Outlook Express attaches a priority icon to the message (assuming that the recipients of the message are using Outlook Express to read their mail) that indicates its relative importance. The high-priority icon has a red flag in front of the envelope, whereas the low-priority icon has an arrow pointing downward.

5. (Optional) To boost the priority of the message, choose Message➪Set Priority and then choose High in the submenu that appears. To decrease the priority of the message, click the Priority button, and choose Low on the submenu.

6. Click the cursor in the body of the message and then type in the text of the message as you would in any text editor or word processor, ending paragraphs and short lines by pressing the Enter key.

When composing the text of the message, keep in mind that you can insert text directly into the body of the message from other documents via the Clipboard (the old Cut, Copy, and Paste commands).

7. (Optional) If you're not sure of some (or all) of the spelling in the text of the body of the message, you can have Outlook Express check the spelling by inserting the cursor at the beginning of the message text and then clicking the Spelling button on the New Message toolbar or by choosing Tools⇨Spelling on the menu bar (or by pressing F7).

When spell-checking the message, Outlook Express flags each word that it cannot find in the dictionary and tries its best to suggest an alternative.

To replace the unknown word in the text with the word suggested in the Change To text box of the Spelling window, click the Change button or, if it's a word that occurs frequently in the rest of the text, click Change All.

To ignore the unknown word and have the spelling checker continue to scan the rest of the text for possible misspellings, click Ignore or, if it's a word that occurs frequently in the rest of the text, click Ignore All.

8. (Optional) To send a file along with your e-mail message, click the Attach button on the New Message toolbar or choose Insert⇨File Attachment on the menu bar; then select the file in the Insert Attachment dialog box and click the Attach button.

When you include a file with a message, an icon for the file appears in a new Attach field immediately below the Subject field above the body of the e-mail message.

9. To send the e-mail message to its recipients, click the Send button on the New Message toolbar or choose File⇨Send Message on the menu bar (or press Ctrl+Enter or Alt+S).

Note that when composing a new message, you can send blind copies of the message to several recipients by filling in the Bcc: field. To display the Bcc: field between the Cc: and Subject: fields, select View⇨All Headers on the Outlook Express new message menu bar. You can fill in this field with the names of the recipients as you do in the Cc: field (*see* Step 3 in the preceding list). When you add names to the Bcc: field rather than to the Cc: field, no recipient sees any other names that you've entered. When you add names to the Cc: field, each recipient sees the names of everyone else to whom you've sent this same message.

If you have more than one e-mail account that you've set up in Outlook Express, the New Message dialog box will contain a From field at the top of the message header. You can use the drop-down button attached to this field to select from which of your e-mail accounts the new message is to be sent.

If you compose e-mail messages when you cannot get online to send them, choose File⇨Send Later from the New Message window menu bar after you finish composing each message. Outlook Express then displays an alert box indicating that the message will be stored in the Outbox and will be sent the next time you click the Send and Receive button. To send the messages stored in the Outbox when you can connect or are connected to the Internet, just click the Send and Receive button on the Outlook Express toolbar.

Adding recipients to the Address Book

Outlook Express makes it easy to maintain an address book (called the Address Book and referred to as Contacts), where you can store the e-mail addresses for all the people you regularly correspond with. If you're switching from some other e-mail program (such as the one that comes with Netscape Navigator), and you've created an address book with that program, you can even import all the addresses into the Address Book, making it unnecessary to re-enter them.

To add a new recipient to the Address Book, follow these steps:

1. Open Outlook Express by clicking the Outlook Express button on the Quick Launch toolbar.

2. Click the Contacts button at the top of the Contacts pane in the lower-left corner of the Outlook Express window and then click New Contact.

    You can also click the Addresses button on the Outlook Express toolbar (Ctrl+Shift+B) to open the Address Book window and then choose File⇨New Contact (Ctrl+N).

3. Fill in the Name information for the new contact in the various name fields and then select the E-Mail Addresses text box, where you type the recipient's e-mail address before clicking the Add button.

When you click the Add button, Outlook Express adds the e-mail address you entered into the list box, automatically designating it as Default E-Mail.

If the person you are adding to the Windows Address Book has more than one e-mail address (as would be the case if, for example, he or she maintains an e-mail account at home with one address and an e-mail account at work with another address), you can add the additional e-mail address.

4. (Optional) Enter the recipient's alternate e-mail address in the E-Mail Addresses text box and then click Add again to add other e-mail addresses for the same recipient.

If you want to make the second e-mail address the default address that Outlook Express automatically uses when you compose a new message, you need to select the second address in the list box and then click the Set as Default button.

To use a contact's alternate e-mail address in a new message, you need to select the person's name in the Select Recipients dialog box and then click the Properties button, where you make the alternate e-mail address the new default with the Set as Default button.

5. Click the OK button to close the Properties dialog box.

If you added the new contact from the Address Book window, Outlook Express returns you to this window, where the contact's name appears, followed by the new default e-mail address.

To import the addresses from an address book created with Eudora, Microsoft Exchange, Microsoft Internet Mail for Windows, or Netscape Navigator, or addresses stored in a comma-separated text file, into the Windows Address Book, follow these steps:

1. Open Outlook Express by clicking the Outlook Express button on the Quick Launch toolbar.

2. Choose File⇨Import⇨Other Address Book from the Outlook Express menu bar to open the Address Book Import Tool dialog box.

3. Click the type of address book you want to import in the list box of the Address Book Import Tool dialog box and then click the Import button.

After Outlook Express imports the names and e-mail addresses of all the contacts in the existing address book, it closes the Windows Address Book Import Tool dialog box and returns you to the Address Book dialog box. The imported contacts now appear in that dialog box.

4. (Optional) To sort the contacts in the Address Book by last names, click the Names button at the top of the first entry. To sort the contacts by e-mail addresses, click the E-mail Address button instead.

5. Click the Close button in the upper-right corner of the Windows Address Book window to close it.

Reading e-mail

When you use Outlook Express as your e-mail program, you read the messages that you receive in an area known as the Inbox. To open the Inbox in Outlook Express and read your e-mail messages, take these steps:

1. Open Outlook Express by clicking the Outlook Express button on the Quick Launch toolbar on the taskbar.

   When browsing Web pages in Internet Explorer, you can also open the Inbox in Outlook Express by clicking the Mail button on the Standard Buttons bar and then choosing Read Mail on the pop-up menu that appears.

2. Click the Send/Recv (for Send and Receive) button on the Outlook Express toolbar, or press Ctrl+M, to have Outlook Express check your Mail server and download any new messages and switch to the Inbox view.

   As soon as you click the Send/Recv button, Outlook Express opens a connection to your Mail server, where it checks for any new messages to download. New messages are then downloaded to your computer. The program also selects the Inbox view so that the Outlook Express pane is replaced with two vertical Inbox panes: the one above, which lists the messages in the Inbox, and the one immediately below, which displays the first part of the text of the currently selected message.

   You can also open this Inbox view either by clicking the Inbox icon in the Folders pane or the hyperlink in the Outlook Express pane on the right that tells you the number of unread Mail messages in your Inbox.

   Descriptions of any new messages appear in bold at the bottom of the list in the upper pane of the Inbox, which is divided into five columns: Priority (indicated by an exclamation mark), Attachments (indicated by the paper clip), From,

Subject, and Received (showing both the date and time that the e-mail message was downloaded on your computer).

Note that mail messages that you haven't yet read are indicated not only by bold type, but also by a sealed-envelope icon in the From column. Mail messages that you *have* read are indicated by an opened-envelope icon.

3. To read one of your new messages, click any column of the description in the upper pane of the Inbox.

   The text of the message that you select appears in the lower-right pane of the Inbox, and the From and Subject information appears on the bar dividing the upper-right pane from the lower-right pane. If the message has one or more files attached to it, a paper clip appears on the right side of this bar.

4. (Optional) To open the file or files attached to the e-mail message with its native program (or at least one that can open the file), click the paper-clip icon and then click the name of the file to open in the pop-up menu. To save the attachments as separate files on your hard drive, click Save Attachments on this pop-up menu (or click File⇨Save Attachments on the Outlook Express menu bar) and then select the folder in which to save the files in the Save Attachments dialog box.

   Sometimes, you may need to get a hard copy of the message to share with other, less fortunate workers in the office who don't have e-mail. (If they do have e-mail, forward the message to them instead, as I cover in optional Step 8.)

5. (Optional) To print the contents of an e-mail message, click the Print button on the Outlook Express toolbar or choose File⇨ Print (Ctrl+P) and then click OK in the Print dialog box.

   Occasionally, an e-mail message will contain some information that you want to be able to reuse in other documents without having to retype it. Rather than having to open the message in the Outlook Express Inbox and then copy the contents to a new document via the Clipboard, you can save it as either a text file or an HTML file (both of which can be opened in a word processor, such as Microsoft Office Word 2003).

6. (Optional) To save the contents of an e-mail message as a separate e-mail message file or as a text file , choose File⇨Save As to open the Save Message As dialog box. Next, choose the folder in which to save the file in the Save In drop-down list box, and the file format in which to save the file in the Save As type drop-down list box (select the Mail [*.eml] option to save it in the e-mail format, Text Files [*.txt] to save it as a text file, or HTML Files [*.htm, *.html] to save it in the Hypertext Markup Language used by Web pages). Then click the Save button.

If the e-mail message uses the High Priority exclamation-mark icon, chances are good that you may have to reply to it right away. You can respond to the message by clicking either the Reply or the Reply All button.

After you click one of these buttons, Outlook Express opens a message window in which

- The sender of the original message is listed as the recipient in the To: field

- The subject of the original message appears in the Subject: field, preceded by the term Re: (regarding)

- The contents of the original message appear in the body of the reply beneath the heading Original Message, followed by the From:, To:, Date:, and Subject: information from the original message

7. (Optional) To reply to the author of the e-mail message, click the Reply button on the Outlook Express toolbar. To send copies of the reply to all the others copied on the original message as well, click the Reply All button instead. Then add the text of your reply above the text of the original message and send the reply (by pressing Ctrl+Enter or Alt+S).

Sometimes, in addition to or instead of replying to the original message, you need to send a copy of it to someone who wasn't listed in the Bcc: or Cc fields. To send a copy to this person, you forward a copy of the original message to the new recipients of your choosing. When you forward a message, Outlook Express copies the Subject: and contents of the original message to a new message, which you then address and send.

8. (Optional) To forward the e-mail message to another e-mail address, click the Forward button on the Outlook Express toolbar. Then fill in the recipient information in the To: and, if applicable, Bcc: or Cc: field; add any additional text of your own above that of the original message; and send the forwarded message on its way (by pressing Ctrl+Enter or Alt+S).

If you ever open an e-mail message and then don't have time to really read through it and digest the meaning, you can, if you'd like, have Outlook Express mark the message as unread to help remind you to reread it at a later date when you have more time. To mark a read e-mail message as unread, click Edit➪Mark as Unread on the Outlook Express menu bar. Outlook then replaces the open-envelope icon in front of the current message with the closed-envelope icon. To temporarily hide all messages in the Inbox except those you haven't yet read, click View➪Current View➪Hide Read Messages on the menu bar. To later redisplay both the read and unread messages in the Inbox, you then click View➪Current View➪Show All Messages.

Also note that as part of the security features in the SP2 update to Windows XP, Outlook Express now automatically blocks the display of all pictures in incoming messages (to prevent the sender from identifying your computer). If you trust the source of the message, you can display the images by clicking the note at the top of body of the e-mail message indicating that the pictures are blocked.

Organizing e-mail

Getting e-mail is great, but it doesn't take long for you to end up with a disorganized mess. If you're anything like me, your Outlook Express Inbox will end up with hundreds of messages, some of which are still unread — and all of which are lumped together in one extensive list.

Outlook Express makes it easy for you to arrange your e-mail messages in folders. To send a bunch of related e-mail messages into a new or existing folder, follow these steps:

1. Open Outlook Express by clicking the Outlook Express button on the Quick Launch toolbar on the taskbar *and* then clicking the Inbox icon in the Folders pane in the upper-left part of the Outlook Express window.

2. Select all the messages that you want to put in the same folder. To select a single message, click the description. To select a continuous series of messages, click the first one and hold down the Shift key as you click the last one. To click multiple messages that aren't in a series, hold down Ctrl as you click the description of each one.

3. After you select the messages that you want to move, choose Edit➪Move To Folder on the Outlook Express menu bar (Ctrl+Shift+V) to open the Move dialog box, or you can just drag the message to the folder.

4. Click the Inbox folder icon and then click the name of the sub-folder into which the selected messages are to be moved. If you need to create a new folder for the selected items, click the New Folder button, type the name in the Folder Name text box, and click OK. Then click the Inbox folder icon before clicking the name of the newly created subfolder.

5. Click OK in the Move dialog box to move the messages into the selected folder.

To verify that the items are now in the correct folder, click the folder icon in the outline (beneath the Inbox icon) that appears in the left pane of the Outlook Express window.

Don't forget that the most basic way to organize your e-mail is by sorting all the messages in the Inbox (or any of the other Outlook Express folders, for that matter) by clicking the column button. For example, if you want to sort the e-mail in your Inbox by subject, click the Subject button at the top of the list. So, too, if you want to sort the messages by the date and time received (from earliest to most recent), you click the Received button at the top of that column.

Deleting e-mail

As you get more and more e-mail in your Inbox, you might want to use the File⇨Folder⇨Compact command to compress the messages, thus freeing up valuable disk space. When you have e-mail in all sorts of different folders, you can compact all the messages by choosing File⇨Folder⇨Compact All Folders instead.

When you have messages (especially those unsolicited ones) that you no longer need to store on your computer hard drive, you can move those messages to the Deleted Items folder by selecting them and then choosing Edit⇨Delete (Ctrl+D). You can then get rid of them for good by right-clicking the Deleted Items icon in the Folders bar and then clicking Yes in the alert box telling you that you're about to permanently delete the selected messages.

If you receive unsolicited messages from advertisers or people whose e-mail you don't want to receive again in the future, click one of the sender's e-mail messages in the Inbox and then select Message⇨Block Sender on the menu bar. You then receive an alert dialog box informing you that the person has been added to your block-senders list and asking you if you now want to remove all messages from the Inbox from that sender. Click the Yes button to remove the messages, or click No to retain them.

To remove someone you've blocked from your Blocked Senders list so that you can once again get e-mail from that person, select Tools⇨Message Rules⇨Block Senders List and then click the name of the e-mail address you want to unblock before you click the Remove button.

To remove messages from the Inbox without permanently getting rid of them, select them and then press the Delete key. They instantly disappear from the Inbox window. If you ever need them again, however, you can display them by clicking the Deleted Items icon in the Outlook Express window left pane.

To get rid of all the items in the Deleted Items folder, right-click the icon in the left pane of the Outlook Express window and then click Empty "Deleted Items" Folder on the icon shortcut menu.

Instant Messaging

Windows Messenger allows you to send instant messages to all
your contacts, making it somewhat equivalent to an online chat.
You can access the instant-messaging service in a number of ways:
from the Start menu on the Windows taskbar, the Notification area
of the Windows taskbar, within Internet Explorer, or from within
Outlook Express.

✓ To open Windows Messenger from the Start menu on the
  taskbar, click Start, point to All Programs, and then click
  Windows Messenger on the continuation menu.

✓ To open Windows Messenger from the Notification area of the
  taskbar, double-click the Messenger icon (the one with the icon
  that looks like a ball on top of a flat pyramid that's supposed to
  look like a person), or right-click it and then choose Open on
  the shortcut menu. (Note that the Messenger icon doesn't show
  up in the Notification area until you click the Expand button
  [<<] to display more icons and until after you've signed up for a
  passport, as I explain in the paragraph following this list.)

✓ To open Windows Messenger from Internet Explorer, click the
  Messenger button on the Standard Buttons toolbar or choose
  Tools➪Windows Messenger on the pull-down menu.

✓ To open Windows Messenger from Outlook Express, choose
  Tools➪Windows Messenger➪Log On from the Outlook Express
  pull-down menu (if you're already logged onto MSN, you click
  Send Instant Message on the continuation menu instead of
  Log On).

The first time that you open Windows Messenger, it takes you
to the Microsoft Passport home page. Before you can use instant
messaging, you must sign up and get a passport. This process
involves assigning yourself an online handle (such as *cooldude500*),
a sign-in name that becomes your e-mail address when combined
with hotmail.com (such as nancy345@hotmail.com), and a password
for logging onto Windows Messenger. To get a Passport account,
open the Welcome screen of the Windows Messenger wizard (using
any of the aforementioned methods) and then click the Next button
to advance to the Get a Free Passport screen, where you click the
Get a Passport button.

After you finish setting up your passport account, you can log on
at any time to Windows Messenger from the Windows Messenger
Wizard. Just click the Next button twice to reach the Provide
Passport Information screen, where you type your sign-in name
and password in the text boxes provided. Then click Next to
advance to the final screen, where you click the Finish button.

Windows closes the Windows Messenger wizard and opens the
Windows Messenger window, similar to the one shown in the following figure.

Adding contacts

After you've got your passport, you're ready to add the contacts
with whom you want to correspond to your Windows Messenger
list. Note that all the contacts that you add to this list must already
have passports. If the person who you want to add to your list
doesn't have a passport, Windows Messenger will send him or her
an e-mail message inviting that person to sign up for one. The
e-mail message even contains a link that takes the recipient to the
Microsoft Passport home page.

To add a contact, follow these steps:

1. Open the Windows Messenger window by right-clicking the
   Messenger icon in the Notification area of the Windows
   taskbar; then choose Open on the shortcut menu.

2. Click the Add a Contact link or choose File⇨Add a Contact on
   the pull-down menus to open the Add a Contact Wizard.

3. By default, Windows Messenger selects the By E-mail Address
   or Sign-in Name radio button to search for new contacts by
   their regular e-mail addresses. If you know the contact's e-mail
   address (meaning that he or she has a passport), click the
   Search for a Contact radio button instead to search for the
   person by name and location.

4. Click Next to advance to the next dialog box.

5. Enter the appropriate search information: the e-mail address, if By E-mail Address or Sign-in Name was selected in Step 3; or the first and last name, physical location, and which directory to search (either the Hotmail Member Directory or your Windows Address Book), if you selected Search for a Contact.

6. Click Next to search for the contact.

   If the contact is located and has a passport, the wizard will display a message to that effect in the next dialog box. If the contact is located by the wizard but doesn't yet have a passport, the wizard will display a message indicating that this is the case and that you can send this person an e-mail inviting him or her to join. To send such an e-mail message, click the Next button and then type your invitation to join to the person in the upper list box. You can also edit the message that's automatically added to yours shown in the lower list box by clicking the Change Language button. When you're satisfied with the message, click Next to send the message.

7. (Optional) To repeat the process outlined in Steps 3 through 6 and add other contacts, click Next.

8. After you've finished adding contacts, click Finish to close the Add a Contact Wizard and return to the Windows Messenger window.

The sign-in names for all the contacts that you successfully added will now appear in the All Contacts section of the Windows Messenger window.

Sending instant messages

After you've added your contact, you're ready for instant messaging. You can check to see whether any of your contacts are logged onto Windows Messenger by double-clicking their names in the All Contacts section of the Windows Messenger window. A dialog box then opens, indicating whether or not this contact is online and ready to accept messages.

To send an instant message to someone in your contacts list who is currently online, click the contact's handle (that is, that contact's instant-messaging online nickname) in the Windows Messenger window and then click the Send an Instant Message link in the I Want To section at the bottom of the Windows Messenger window. Doing this opens a Conversation dialog box with the contact's handle on the title bar. To send a message to this contact (up to 400 words), start typing the message text at the cursor in the box at the bottom of this dialog box. When you finish typing the text, click the Send button to the right or press Enter.

As soon as you send your message, your contact's computer beeps, and your handle appears in a flashing button on his or her Windows taskbar. When the contact clicks this button, a Conversation dialog box with your handle in the title opens. The contact can then respond to your initial message by typing one of his or her own and then clicking the Send button.

The contact's response will then immediately show up in that person's Conversation dialog box on your computer, and you can respond to his or her response, thus starting what can prove to be an almost real-time chat (some delay may occur if your contact's responses are rather lengthy and your Internet connection is slow).

When you close Windows Messenger by clicking the Close button, the Messenger displays an alert box indicating that although you're closing the window, Windows Messenger will continue to run in the background on the Windows taskbar so that you can continue to receive notifications and messages.

If your computer and your contacts' computers are equipped with microphones and Web cameras, you can start a voice or video conversation with them. To start a voice conversation, click the Start a Voice Conversation link in the I Want To section of the Windows Messenger window. To communicate both by voice and video, click the Start a Video Conversation link in this same area.

Retrieving e-mail via Windows Messenger

You can also use Windows Messenger in conjunction with Hotmail to send and retrieve regular e-mail messages. By using your Hotmail mailbox, you can retrieve your e-mail messages from any computer that has Internet access.

To use Windows Messenger to send or retrieve e-mail through the Microsoft Hotmail service, click the More hyperlink in I Want To section of the Messenger window and then click Go to My E-mail Inbox on the pop-up menu. Doing this connects you to the Internet and opens the Inbox page for your Hotmail account on the MSN Hotmail Web site. You can then read your e-mail messages, reply to messages, and even compose new e-mail, using the buttons at the top of the page.

When you're logged onto Windows Messenger on your computer, Windows Messenger lets you know when new e-mail messages arrive in your Hotmail inbox by beeping at you and displaying a ScreenTip message (saying that you have new e-mail) above the Messenger icon on the Windows status bar.

Part III

Windows Accessories

Part III introduces you to the Windows Accessories. Accessories are little extra programs thrown into the Windows XP operating system that make Windows more versatile, as well as just a bit safer and easier to use. Along with the more mundane and practical accessories, such as Disk Cleanup and System Monitor, designed to keep your computer system humming, you'll find some new, fun ones, such as Windows Movie Maker, that will definitely help you enjoy your computer a heck of a lot more.

In this part . . .

Accessibility

The Accessibility accessories are utilities that make it easier for people with less-than-perfect physical dexterity to operate a computer. When you click All Programs⇨Accessories⇨Accessibility on the Start menu, Windows displays a continuation menu with the following menu items:

- **Accessibility Wizard:** Steps you through configuration settings that determine the smallest size of fonts and other items that appear on-screen.

- **Magnifier:** Makes the screen more readable for the visually impaired. The magnifier creates a separate window at the top of the screen that displays a magnified image of a portion of your screen. When you open the utility, the Magnifier Settings dialog box enables you to determine the necessary degree of magnification; you also use the dialog box to turn the feature on and off.

- **Narrator:** Enables you to select settings for the Windows text-to-speech utility that reads aloud text in Notepad, WordPad, Control Panel programs and Internet Explorer 6, as well as on the Windows desktop and in the Windows setup program.

- **On-Screen Keyboard:** Displays a keyboard on-screen that you can use to input characters either with a mouse or some other sort of switch-type input device.

- **Utility Manager:** Displays the Utility Manager dialog box, which shows which Accessibility options are currently running and enables you to designate under what conditions to automatically start the Magnifier.

Accessing Your Accessories

To access any of the many Windows XP accessories, click the Start button on the Windows taskbar and then click All Programs⇨ Accessories on the Start menu that appears. Clicking the Accessories item displays a continuation menu beginning with five categories (Accessibility, Communications, Entertainment, Microsoft Interactive Training, and System Tools), followed by a list of individual accessories (Address Book, Calculator, Command Prompt, and so on).

To launch an accessory from a particular category on the Accessories continuation menu, highlight the category folder on the Accessories menu and then click the particular accessory program icon on the submenu that appears. To launch a particular accessory from this menu, simply click that name on the Accessories continuation menu.

 If you find that some of the accessories that I cover in this part aren't installed on your computer as part of the original Windows XP installation, you can add them. All you need to do is use the Add or Remove Programs hyperlink in the Control menu. **See** "Adding or Removing Programs" in Part I for more.

Address Book

The Address Book enables you to keep an online card file for all the business and personal contacts that you keep. E-mail programs, such as Outlook Express 6 and Microsoft Office Outlook 2003, can access the e-mail addresses that you keep in the Address Book. When you choose All Programs⇨Accessories⇨Address Book on the Start menu, Windows opens the Address Book window, where you can add and edit the contacts that you track.

To add a new contact, click File⇨New Contact on the Address Book menu bar or press Ctrl+N and then fill in the pertinent information on the various tabs of the new Properties dialog box before you click OK. To edit an existing contact, double-click the name in the Address Book window, or click it and then click File⇨Properties or press Alt+Enter to open the contact's Properties dialog box.

When you open a contact's Properties dialog box, the first tab (Summary) displays all the information that you've entered for that contact. You can then click the individual tabs and make changes to the information stored in the individual fields.

Calculator

When you click All Programs⇨Accessories⇨Calculator on the Start menu, Windows opens the Calculator. The Calculator accessory supplies you with an on-screen calculator that you can use to perform all sorts of arithmetic computations on the fly.

The following is a list of the buttons and their functions found on the calculator:

✔ **Numbers 0-9:** To enter a value, click the number buttons or type the number from the keyboard or numeric keypad.

✔ **Backspace:** Click to backspace over a particular numeric entry to delete it.

✔ **CE:** Click to clear an entry.

✔ **C:** Click to clear the calculator of all entries and calculations.

✔ **+:** Click after entering a value to add one value to another.

✔ **+/–:** Click after entering a value to change the sign. If the value is positive, clicking this button makes it negative. If the value is negative, clicking this button makes it positive. Note that to subtract one value from another, you need make the value you want to subtract negative and then add it to the positive value.

✔ ***:** Click after entering a value to multiply one value by another.

✔ **/:** Click after entering a value to divide one value by another.

Note that the preceding operator buttons (+, *, and /) also function as subtotal buttons, enabling you to perform running calculations with mixed operators.

The other calculator buttons and their purposes are as follows:

✔ **=:** Click to get the total of an addition, subtraction, multiplication, or division calculation.

✔ **sqrt:** Enter a value and then click this button to get the square root of that value.

✔ **%:** Click to convert the current value into a percentage by dividing it by 100.

✔ **1/x:** Click to convert the current value into a fraction by dividing 1 by it.

✔ **MS:** To store a value or the result of a calculation into the calculator's memory, enter the value or perform the calculation and then click this button.

✔ **M+:** To add a value or calculation to those already stored in the calculator's memory, enter the value or perform the calculation and then click this button.

✔ **MR:** Click to enter a value stored in the calculator's memory.

✔ **MC:** Click to clear the calculator's memory.

If you're an engineer and need access to enigmatic functions, such as sine, cosine, and tangent, you can switch the simple bank-balance version of the calculator to a fancy-Dan scientific calculator by selecting View⇨Scientific on the menu bar. You can return to the regular calculator by selecting View⇨Standard.

Command Prompt

When you click All Programs⇨Accessories⇨Command Prompt on the Start menu, Windows opens the Command Prompt window, with a DOS-like command prompt where you can enter MS-DOS and UNIX commands. *See* "Using the Command Prompt" in Part I for more on the Command Prompt window.

Communications

When you click All Programs⇨Accessories⇨Communications on the Start menu, Windows displays a continuation menu with options for getting connected to other people and to computers. You can use the Network Setup Wizard or Network Connections items to set up your computer as part of a LAN (local area network) so that you can share files and resources, such as networked printers and Internet connections. You can use the HyperTerminal program to connect with computers running other operating systems and to send and receive text and data files, and if you're running Windows XP Professional, you can use Remote Desktop Connection to connect to another computer desktop and run programs as though you were sitting in front of the remote computer monitor.

Networking

When you select the Network Setup Wizard on the Communications Accessories submenu, Windows starts the Network Setup Wizard, which helps you set up a network between two or more computers. Such a network enables all your home computers to share files, printers, and a single Internet connection. Before you can use the Network Setup Wizard to set up your home network, you must make sure that each computer is equipped with a network adapter (most often in the form of a network interface card, or NIC) and that the computers are all properly cabled together.

To network two computers, you need only to connect a cable between the two network adapters. To network more than two computers, you have to purchase a network hub, which interconnects all the network adapters. To add a printer to the home network, the printer must be equipped with a separate network adapter and be connected to the network hub. In addition, you need to install the printer *as a network printer* on each of the networked computers. *See* "Printing" in Part I for details on installing a network printer.

Note that at least one of the computers in the home network *has* to be running Windows XP in order to provide the necessary networking software (and all the other computers on the network must be running at least Windows 95). Make sure that if only one of your computers has Windows XP installed on it, this computer is also the one that has a modem and is the one on which your connection to the Internet is installed. This computer acts as the server that coordinates all the networking activities for your home network.

The Network Setup Wizard walks you through the steps for creating an identity for your home network, indicating whether your computer has a high-speed connection to the Internet, and takes you through the steps for installing the Internet Connection Sharing software that's needed if you want to share your Internet connection with the other computers on the home network.

Network Connections

When you select Network Connections on the Communications Accessories submenu, Windows opens the Network Connections dialog box, where you view or modify the properties of an existing network connection, select an alternate network connection, or create a new connection to the Internet or a local area network.

To get information on an existing network connection, click the icon in the Network Connections window and then click File⇨Properties on the menu bar. To select another network connection, such as a dial-up connection when your laptop computer isn't directly connected to the company's local area network, double-click the connection icon in the Network Connections window.

To create a new network connection, click the Create a New Connection hyperlink in the navigation pane of the Network Connections window or click File⇨New Connection on the menu bar to open the Network Connection Wizard. This wizard enables you to set up any of three different connections types: Internet connection using your telephone line or broadband connection (with a DSL/cable modem); connection to a private network, such as the company's local area network, from home (using a phone line or a virtual private network over the Internet); or a direct connection (using a parallel or serial cable or an infrared port).

When using the Network Connection Wizard, you must be able to specify the necessary logins, passwords, and, in the case of phone connections, telephone numbers. Get this information from your Internet service provider's technical support people or your company's Internet and network support personnel before you attempt to create a new network connection.

Remote Desktop Connection

You can use the Remote Desktop Connection Communications accessory to share the desktop of your computer remotely. You can use this feature for a variety of reasons:

- ✔ **Working from home:** Access your work computer from a home computer over the Internet, giving you access to all of its programs and resources.

- ✔ **Collaborating:** Access the program's and documents on a co-worker's computer from your own computer over a LAN or the Internet, enabling you to directly review and edit the work you collaborate on.

- ✔ **Sharing a single computer:** Enable different users sharing the same computer to maintain separate program sessions.

To use Remote Desktop, each computer needs to be running Windows XP Professional and have access to a Local Area Network via network connection, modem, or Virtual Private Network (VPN) connection. Each computer must also have Remote Desktop Connection (formerly known as Terminal Services Client) installed.

Before you can use the Remote Desktop Connection accessory on your computer, you must enable the machine for desktop sharing. Note that in order to do this, you must be logged on to your computer as a user who has Computer Administrator privileges (**see** "User Accounts" in Part IV for details).

To enable your computer for Remote Desktop Connection, follow these steps:

1. Open the System Control panel by clicking Start and Control Panel. If the Control panel is in Category view, click Performance and Maintenance in the Pick a Category dialog box, followed by the See Basic Information about Your System or the System link in the Performance and Maintenance dialog box (if the Control panel is in Classic View, simply double-click the System icon).

2. Click the Remote tab in the System Properties dialog box.

3. Click the Allow Users to Connect Remotely to This Computer check box.

4. (Optional) To specify which users on the computer can connect to it remotely, click the Select Remote Users button and then add their names in the Remote Desktop Users dialog box.

   Doing this ensures that no one else can access your computer but those on the list.

5. Click OK in the System Properties dialog box to close it.

After you enable remote desktop sharing on your computer, you can gain access to its desktop by choosing Remote Desktop connection on the Communications submenu (Start⇨All Programs⇨ Accessories⇨Communications⇨Remote Desktop Connection). Windows opens the Remote Desktop Connection dialog box, where you select the name of your computer. To expand this dialog box to include Logon settings where you specify not only the computer name, but also your user name, password, and the domain the computer is on (if your network uses domains), click the Options > button.

After filling in your logon information, click the Connect button to connect to the computer whose name you specify in the Computer drop-down list box. Windows then displays the desktop of the remote computer full-screen on your computer, giving you full access to all of its programs and resources.

Note that the name of the remote computer appears in a bar at the top of your computer's screen to let you know that you're looking at a remote computer's desktop and not the one of the computer you are using. This bar contains Minimize, Restore, and Close buttons on the right side. Click the Restore button to view the remote computer's desktop in a less-than-full-size window (whose title bar then has the name of the remote computer, followed by Remote Desktop) that you can then move the local desktop. When you finish accessing the remote computer, you simply have to click the Close button to end the Remote Desktop Connection session. When you click Close, the Disconnect Windows Session alert dialog box appears, informing you that you are about to disconnect your remote sharing session. Click the OK button to close this dialog box and terminate the remote sharing.

Remote Desktop Connection automatically locks the desktop of the remote computer during a remote sharing session (so that no one at the remote location can come along and try to start using the computer at the same time as you). To unlock the remote computer during a remote sharing session so that you have local access to its desktop, you need to press Ctrl+Alt+Delete at the same time.

If you share your computer with other users, and you turn on Fast Desktop Sharing, you can give them access to the computer without having to shut down your remote sharing session during the interruption. For example, suppose you're logged onto your work computer from your home computer, and someone in the household needs to log on and send an important e-mail before you finish the remote desktop sharing. With Fast Desktop Sharing enabled, you can let that person log on (Start⇨Log Off⇨Switch User) and send the vital e-mail; then, after he or she finishes and logs off (Start⇨Log Off⇨Log Off), you log back on and resume using the remotely shared desktop as though nothing had disrupted your session. To turn on Fast Desktop Switching for the users on your computer, open the User Accounts Control panel (*see* "User Accounts" in Part IV for details); then click the Change the Way Users Log On or Off link and click the User Fast User Switching check box to insert a check mark in it before you click the Apply Options button.

Entertainment

Selecting the Entertainment option on the Accessories continuation menu leads to a further submenu that contains the following: Sound Recorder, Volume Control, and Windows Media Player (*see* "Playing Music, Video, and Movies" in Part I for detailed information on using Windows Media Player).

Sound Recorder

The Sound Recorder accessory enables you to record and save sound files with a microphone connected to your sound card. To record your voice, click the Record button (the one with the red dot). To stop the recording, click the Stop button (the one with the rectangle). To play back the recording, click the Play button (the one with a single triangle pointing to the right).

To save a sound file, click File⇨Save on the Sound Recorder window menu bar. Note that Windows XP saves your sound files in its native WAV file format, using the PCM codec (coder/decoder software that can compress and uncompress audio and video data). The Microsoft PCM codec enables you to play audio files at a one kilohertz rate on sound cards that support another rate, so 8-bit cards can play 16-bit audio by reducing the sound quality.

If you want to save your sound recordings with another codec, such as MPEG Layer-3 (designed for creating CD-quality files for use on Web pages on an intranet or the Internet at bit rates between 8 and 32 kilobytes per second), you need to select File⇨Save As on the window menu bar and then click the Change button at the bottom of the Save As dialog box. Doing this displays the Sound Selection dialog box, where you can select a new codec in the Format pull-down menu, as well as a new bit rate in the Attributes pull-down menu.

You can add sound files you record with the Sound Recorder to text documents that you create with the Windows WordPad utility or Microsoft Office Word 2003 using the Windows Clipboard. You can then play back these sounds right from within the text documents by double-clicking the speaker icon that Windows inserts in the document or right-clicking it and then selecting Sound Recorder

Document Object⇨Play on the shortcut menu. You might do this to add verbal editing instructions to a document so that the person who does the editing can listen to the instructions prior to making the changes.

Volume Control

The Volume Control accessory on the Entertainment Accessories menu enables you to set the volume and balance for your speakers when playing audio CDs or system sounds, or when recording sound files in the Sound Recorder accessory with your microphone. It also enables you to set the volume and balance for recording devices, including CD Audio and your computer microphone.

When you first open the Volume Control window, it shows you the playback volume controls. This Volume Control window (shown in the following figure) is divided into sections that control the volume and balance of individual playback sound components, such as Wave, SW Synth, and CD Player, with a section at the beginning that controls the overall speaker volume and balance.

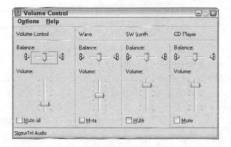

Note that the controls that appear in the Volume Control dialog box on your computer may differ from those shown in the previous figure, as the options depend upon the type of sound card in your computer and the Volume options selected for your system.

To change the volume for a particular component, drag the Volume slider up (to increase volume) or down (to decrease volume). To change the balance for a component, drag the Balance slider to the left (to increase the relative volume in the left speaker) or to the right (to increase the relative volume of the right speaker).

To adjust the volume and balance for recording sound components, click Options⇨Properties on the Volume Control window menu bar and then click the Recording radio button before you select OK. Windows then opens the Recording Control window, with Volume and Balance sliders for each of the recording sound components in your computer system.

When you first open the Volume Control window, it may not display sections for all the sound components of your computer system. To add (or remove) sections from this window, click Options⇨ Properties; then, in the Show the Following Volume Controls list box, click the empty check box to add a check mark to each additional component that you want to appear in the Volume Controls list. If you want to hide the controls of a particular component, click the selected check box to remove the check mark.

You can use this method to display and hide both the playback sound components (shown in the Volume Control window) and the recording sound components. Just click the appropriate radio button (Playback or Recording) in the Adjust Volume For section of the Properties dialog box before you make changes to the check box items in the list box located beneath the "Show the Following Volume Controls" heading in this dialog box.

Microsoft Interactive Training

The Microsoft Interactive Training option on the Accessories submenu gives you access to its Step by Step Interactive (SBSI) audio training on using Windows XP. This training consists of a variety of units (Using Microsoft Interactive Training, Getting Started, Working with Your Computer, Using the Internet, Working in a Network Environment, and Maintaining and Optimizing Your Computer). Each of these units consists of a variety of different lessons with their own topical exercises that you can access sequentially or in any order that fits your needs. Each exercise uses audio and graphics and is fully interactive, automatically pausing between explanations to let you follow each outlined step.

To use the Microsoft Interactive Training, click Start⇨All Programs⇨ Accessories⇨Microsoft Interactive Training⇨Microsoft Interactive Training to open the Course window, which contains an outline of all the units and lessons.

For general instructions on using the interactive training, click the Expand button (the one with the plus sign) in front of Using Microsoft Interactive Training unit and Introduction lesson until you see the How to Use This Product exercise. Double-click this exercise's topic icon to open a Microsoft Windows SBSI - Audio window, complete with the Dashboard dialog box, which contains playback controls for pausing and playing its contents.

To select a new lesson and start a new exercise, simply locate it in the outline in the Course window and then double-click the exercise's topic icon.

Notepad

The Notepad option on the Accessories submenu offers a simple text file editor that you can use to read, edit, and print text files (such as those last-minute README files that seem to accompany all your software).

Notes about using the Notepad accessory:

✔ Text files composed in Notepad use 10-point Lucida Console as the default font, with very simple formatting. (You can change fonts and font sizes by clicking Format⇨Font on the Notepad menu bar and then selecting the new font, font style, and size in the Font dialog box.)

✔ Use Notepad to compose files whenever you know that the document must be saved in a true ASCII-type text file or whenever you're not sure whether the recipient's computer is equipped with a word processor capable of opening and reading a file that's been truly word-processed, such as with Word or WordPad (*see* "WordPad" later in this part for details).

✔ Notepad is not your typical word processor; if you don't press Enter to start a new line or paragraph when typing, it just keeps on going, and going, and going. Notepad does this because it is first and foremost a text editor for editing programming files; carriage returns signify a new line of code.

✔ When a file sports the spiral-bound notebook icon, you can tell that it has been saved as a Notepad file and will automatically open Notepad when you open the icon.

Program Compatibility Wizard

Use the Program Compatibility Wizard on the Accessories submenu when you've upgraded to Windows XP and are experiencing problems with a program that worked with the previous Windows version. The wizard walks you through the steps for locating and then running the program, using a compatibility mode designed for the earlier version Windows.

If you're still experiencing problems with your program after running the Program Compatibility Wizard, contact the program's manufacturer about an upgrade. At this point, almost all software companies have created Windows XP–compatible versions of their programs.

Scanner and Camera Wizard

The Scanner and Camera Wizard on the Accessories submenu enables you to transfer images from digital scanners or cameras that you've connected to your computer onto your hard disk. To use this accessory, first connect your scanner and or digital camera (usually with a USB cable, using a USB port on your computer) and then select Start⇨All Programs⇨Accessories⇨Scanner and Camera Wizard (often, a dialog box enabling you to choose the Scanner and Camera Wizard automatically appears as soon as you connect the device to your computer).

When connected to a digital camera, the wizard scans all the pictures in camera's memory and then walks you through the steps for selecting pictures you want to copy and the folder on your hard disk into which to copy them. It also enables you to select a group filename for the pictures (such as Disneyworld Vacation), to which it then appends sequential numbers (this makes identifying the photos much easier than when they have all numeric filenames).

When connected to a scanner, the wizard takes you through the steps of actually scanning an image with your digital scanner. Depending upon the type of scanner you're using, you can select the picture type (Color, Grayscale, Black and White or Text, or Custom) and preview the image (so that your final scan only contains the part of the image you want).

After the wizard finishes copying the selected camera pictures or scanning your images, its wizard gives you a choice between publishing the digital images to the Web, ordering prints of the images from the Internet, or doing nothing with them (to print the image from your own printer, all you have to do is open the folder that contains them and then click the <u>Print the Selected Pictures</u> link in the folder's Pictures Tasks pane).

Paint

The Paint option on the Accessories submenu offers a simple drawing program with which you can create original graphics or edit bitmapped graphics that you get with Windows XP or other Windows-based programs.

When you select the Paint accessory, Windows opens an empty Paint window that contains a palette of artist tools on the left side and a palette of colors on the bottom.

To open a bitmap file with an existing graphic to edit, click File⇨ Open on the menu bar (or press Ctrl+O) and then select the filename. To create your own original masterpiece, select a drawing tool and have at it!

You can use the Paint accessory to create your own wallpaper designs for the background of the Windows desktop. Just follow these simple steps:

1. After you finish drawing a new graphic or editing an existing one, save it by clicking File⇨Save on the Paint menu bar.

   If necessary, give your new or modified creation a filename.

2. Click File⇨Set As Background (Tiled) or File⇨Set As Background (Centered) from the menu bar. (Choose the Tiled command if you're working with a less-than-full-screen picture and want Windows to replicate it so that it fills the entire screen.)

As soon as you select one of these Set As Background commands, Windows XP immediately makes your wonderful artwork the backdrop against which all further Windows actions take place.

System Tools

A bunch (and I mean a *bunch*) of utilities for keeping your computer system in tip-top shape are located under the System Tools option on the Accessories submenu.

On the System Tools continuation menu, you find the following powerful utilities, which go a long way toward enabling you to spend quality time with your computer:

✔ **Backup:** Enables you to make, compare, or restore backup copies of selected files and folders on either disks or tape. Use this utility to maintain copies of all the files you can't live without, in case (knock on wood) anything ever happens to your computer or the hard drive.

✔ **Character Map:** Enables you to copy any character in a particular font (including those symbols and dingbats you can't insert directly from the keyboard) into the Clipboard.

✔ **Disk Cleanup:** Saves disk space by locating unnecessary files, which you can select for deletion. (Do not delete a file unless you are certain that it's not required by other applications.)

✔ **Disk Defragmenter:** Defragments your hard drive, which means that your files are rearranged so that they use contiguous blocks. This process usually speeds up your computer considerably and is necessary if you use the Media Player.

✔ **File and Settings Transfer Wizard:** Opens the Files and Settings Transfer Wizard, which walks you through the steps of transferring files and settings from an old computer to a new one.

✔ **Scheduled Tasks:** Task Scheduler is a tool that runs in the background every time you start Windows. The Scheduled Tasks accessory enables you to schedule tasks (such as run Disk Defragmenter) daily, weekly, monthly, or at certain times, such as in the middle of the night, when your computer is idle. You can change the schedule for, or turn off, an existing task and customize how a task will run at the scheduled time. *See* "Scheduled Tasks" later in this part to discover how to get these things done.

✔ **System Information:** Tells you everything you ever wanted to know (and even some things you didn't) about your computer system.

✔ **System Restore:** Enables you to return your computer settings to those used at an earlier time. Use this accessory to create a restore point (before you add some new software), and then, if things get messed up when you later add some new software, use System Restore to put your system settings back to the way they were at the time you created the restore point. *See* "System Restore" later in this part for details.

✔ **Security Center:** Opens the Security Center control panel, where you can check and change the Firewall, Automatic Updates, and Virus Protection settings for your computer. *See* "Security Center" in Part IV for details.

Character Map

The Character Map System Tools accessory enables you to copy any character in a particular font (including those symbols and dingbats you can't insert directly from the keyboard) into the Clipboard. From there, you can insert the character into your current text file.

To copy characters to and from the Clipboard by using the Character Map accessory, choose All Programs⇨Accessories⇨ System Tools⇨Character Map from the Start menu to open the Character Map dialog box. Then follow these steps:

1. Choose the font containing the character or characters you want to copy in the Font drop-down list box of the Character Map dialog box. The available characters in the chosen font appear in the viewing area of the dialog box.

2. Select the characters in the font that you want to copy to the Clipboard by double-clicking them or by clicking them and then clicking the Select button. (A larger version of a particular character appears as soon as you click a character to select it.)

3. Click the Copy button to actually copy the selected characters (now proudly displayed in the Characters to Copy text box) to the Clipboard.

4. Switch to the program containing the open text file where you want the copied characters to appear.

5. Position the insertion point at the place in the document text where the copied characters are to be inserted and then select Edit⇨Paste from the menu bar or press Ctrl+V.

In Windows XP, the Character Map accessory enables you to insert a character from any font into document text, regardless of the font chosen for that document. This means that your Wingdings font character chosen in the Character Map dialog box won't turn to the Times New Roman equivalent when you insert it into a text block formatted with the Times New Roman font.

Scheduled Tasks

The Scheduled Tasks accessory on the System Tools continuation menu starts each time you crank up Windows XP, where it dutifully runs in the background. When the Scheduled Tasks utility is running, a tiny icon of a window with a red clock appears next to the real clock on the taskbar.

Selecting All Programs⇨Accessories⇨System Tools⇨Scheduled Tasks on the Start menu opens the Scheduled Tasks window. To schedule a task in the Scheduled Tasks window with the Scheduled Task Wizard, follow these steps:

1. In the list of tasks, double-click the Add Scheduled Task icon at the top of the list of scheduled tasks to open the Scheduled Task Wizard.

2. Click the Next button or press Enter to display the second dialog box of the Scheduled Task Wizard, where you select the program to run.

3. In the list box, click the name of the program you want scheduled to run and then choose the Next button or press Enter to open the third dialog box, where you indicate how often the task should be performed.

4. If you want, enter your own name for the scheduled task in the text box at the top of the dialog box and then select the radio button (Daily, Weekly, Monthly, One Time Only, When My Computer Starts, or When I Log On) indicating when you want the task automatically performed. Then click the Next button or press Enter to display the fourth dialog box of the wizard, where you select the start time and date for the scheduled task.

5. Depending upon what interval option you select in Step 4, enter a beginning time in the Start Time text box or select the time with the spinner buttons; then designate a starting date in the Start Date text box or select it from the drop-down list (only applicable when you select the Weekly or Monthly intervals). Click the Next button or press Enter to display the last dialog box of the Scheduled Task Wizard.

6. Type your user name in the Enter the User Name text box and your optional password in both the Enter the Password and Confirm Password text boxes before you click Next or press Enter.

7. If you want to further configure your scheduled task, select the Open Advanced Properties for This Task When I Click Finish check box before you click the Finish button or press Enter. If you don't need to use the advanced options, just click the Finish button or press Enter without selecting this check box.

When you select the Open Advanced Properties for This Task When I Click Finish check box in the last dialog box of the Scheduled Task Wizard, Windows opens a Properties dialog box for the selected task. This Properties dialog box contains three tabs, which have the following options:

✔ **Task:** Use the options on the Task tab to change the program file to be executed by typing the pathname in the Run text box or by browsing to the program file location on your computer or network.

✔ **Schedule:** Use the options on the Schedule tab to change the time and date for a task and to access options to further refine the task schedule.

✔ **Settings:** Use the options on the Settings tab to define settings for the task upon completion, during idle time, and when power management is a consideration (when using a laptop).

Note that you can access the advanced properties for a task at any time after scheduling it by right-clicking the task in the Scheduled Tasks window and then choosing Properties from the shortcut menu.

Also, you can remove a scheduled task by selecting the task and pressing the Delete key or by clicking the task in the Scheduled Tasks window and then clicking the Delete This Item hyperlink in the window navigation pane and Yes in the alert box asking you to confirm removal of the task to the Recycle Bin.

Make sure that the system date and time for your computer are accurate. The Scheduled Tasks utility relies on this information to know when to run tasks that you schedule.

System Restore

System Restore enables you to turn back the clock on your computer system. For example, say that you're about to add some antivirus software program that you suspect will change a number of system settings. Before installing and using this software, you can use the System Restore accessory to create a restore point. That way, in the unlikely event that you find that the new software destabilizes your computer when it changes your system settings, you can remove the offending software (with the Add or Remove feature — *see* "Adding or Removing Programs" in Part I) and then use the System Restore accessory to go back to systems settings in effect at the restore point (that is, before the new software had a chance to mess with them).

When you click the Start button, point at All Programs⇨Accessories⇨ System Tools and then click System Restore to open the welcome screen of the System Restore window.

To create a restore point from this opening screen, follow these steps:

1. Click the Create a Restore Point radio button and then click Next or press Enter.

2. Enter a descriptive name for the new restore point in the Restore Point Description text box; then click the Create button.

    When creating this name, make sure that you enter a name that clearly indicates to you the current state of your computer, as in "Prior to ACME Anti-Virus Install."

    When Windows finishes creating this restore point, the date, time, and name of the restore point appear below the (grayed-out) Restore Point Description text box in the System Restore screen. If you decide that you want to remove this point, click the Undo button to the immediate right of this information.

3. Click the Close button to close the System Restore accessory and return to the Windows operating system.

After you create a restore point for your Windows settings, you can restore your system to that point by taking these steps:

1. Launch the System Restore accessory by clicking Start and then choosing All Programs⇨Accessories⇨System Tools⇨ System Restore, click the Restore My Computer to an Earlier Time radio button, and then click Next or press Enter.

    The System Restore utility then opens a second screen, where you select the restore point to use in the restoration by indicating the date and time and selecting that name.

2. Choose the date of the restore point by clicking it in the calendar shown on the left side of this screen under the heading "Click a day."

   If the date of the restore point isn't in the current month, click the backward button (marked with a lesser than symbol: <) at the upper-left of the calendar showing the current date.

3. If you created more than one restore point at different times on the same day, click the time and name of the restore point you want to use in the list box under the heading "On this List, click a Restore Point."

4. Click the Next button to display the screen that tells you what changes will be undone when you use the selected restore point and warning you to save all your work and close all open programs before beginning the restore.

5. Click the Next button in this screen to restore your system settings to the date and time of the selected restore point.

   As soon as you click Restore, the screen displays a bar showing the Windows progress in restoring your system settings. As soon as Windows finishes restoring your settings, it will automatically restart your computer so that the newly restored settings are put into effect. Windows will then display a System Restore screen indicating that your system settings were successfully restored.

6. Click the OK button at the bottom of the Restoration Complete screen in the System Restore window to close the System Restore accessory.

Should you use System Restore only to discover that the restore point you selected made Windows XP run even worse than it did before you did the restoration (heaven forbid!), you can undo the restoration by launching System Restore and then clicking the Undo My Last Restoration radio button at the bottom of the opening screen before clicking Next.

Windows Explorer

When you select Start⇨ All Programs⇨Accessories⇨Windows Explorer, Windows opens the My Documents window with the Folders Explorer Bar displayed (or better yet, you right-click the Start button and then click Explore on its shortcut menu). Rather than go through all that trouble, you can do the same thing more simply by clicking the Start button and then clicking My Documents on the Start menu and, when the My Documents window opens, clicking the Folders button on the Standard Buttons toolbar. *See* "My Documents" in Part I.

Windows Movie Maker

You can use the Windows Movie Maker program to capture video and audio clips, which you can then edit and arrange into your very own movies. You can play these movie files on your computer or distribute them to family, friends, and colleagues by e-mail so that they can play them on their computers.

Launch Windows Movie Maker by selecting Start⇨All Programs⇨ Accessories⇨Windows Movie Maker. The Windows Movie Maker program opens the program window full-screen, similar to the one shown in the following figure.

Collections area   Preview

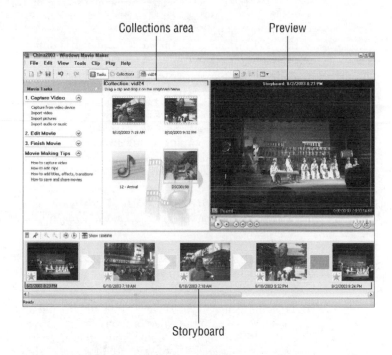

Storyboard

The Movie Maker window is divided into several different sections:

✔ A Movie Task area containing links to all the common Movie Maker tasks. This area is subdivided into three major tasks: Capture Video, for importing video clips into a collection; Edit Movie, for adding video effects, transitions, and titles; and Finish Movie, for rendering the final movie so that you can save it on your computer, send in an e-mail message, upload it to a Web site, or transfer it to a tape on a digital video camera.

✔ A collections area showing thumbnails of the various still graphic images, video clips and audio clips in that collection that you can add to your movie by dragging them to the storyboard area (to select a new collection, click its name in the Collections drop-down list box above).

✔ A work area that either contains the storyboard view (the default), indicating the progression of the movie video clips, or the timeline view (View⇨Timeline or Ctrl+T), indicating the order and duration of both the video and audio (in separate tracks).

✔ A preview area that displays whatever video image or clip is selected in the collections area. You can also use this area to preview the movie that you're putting together by clicking the various control buttons (which use the standard VCR-control symbols) or by dragging the slider bar located under the preview window.

Assembling your clips

To create your movie, you can either import graphic images and sound files into the collections area (Ctrl+I) or, if you can attach a movie camera to your computer, you can digitally record the video and audio clips that you need for your movie project from videotape that you've recorded (Ctrl+R).

Editing the elements in your movie

To assemble your audio and video clips, you sequence them in the work area in one of two views:

✔ Choose the Storyboard view (View⇨Storyboard) to add video clips or still graphics to the movie. You can also use this view to check and alter the order and duration of these video elements.

✔ Choose the Timeline view (View⇨Timeline) to add audio clips to the track beneath the video or to create transitions between the various video clips (or both). You can also use this view to change the sequencing of the audio clips in relation to the video elements in the movie.

To preview your edits to get an idea of how they will play in the final version of the movie, choose the Play⇨Play/Pause command on the menu bar or click the Play button on the controls under the Preview area (the one with the triangle pointing to the right). To pause the movie, press the spacebar or click the Pause button in the preview controls (the one with the two vertical bars). To save your editing work, choose File➪Save Project (Ctrl+S) and give the project a new filename. Windows Movie Maker automatically appends the filename extension MSWMM (for Microsoft Windows Movie Maker) to whatever filename you give the project.

Creating the final movie

When you finish your edits and are satisfied with the final version, you need to convert your Windows Movie Maker project into a movie that Windows Media Player can use. To do this, choose File➪Save Movie File on the menu bar (Ctrl+P) to open the Save Movie Wizard (be sure that you don't use File➪Save Project, because that action saves the project file only for playing in Windows Movie Maker).

In the initial Save Movie Wizard dialog box, choose the movie location (My Computer, Recordable CD, E-Mail, The Web, or DV Camera) and then click the Next button.

Then, if prompted for it, enter the movie title (as in *Land of Snows*) in the Enter a File Name for Your Saved Movie text box and any other pertinent information (such as the place to save the move on your hard disk when you select My Computer as the location and the name for the CD when you select Recordable CD).

Note that when saving the movie to your hard disk, the Save Movie Wizard also prompts you to select the video quality (which directly affects its file size). By default, the wizard selects Best Quality for Playback on My Computer. If space is at a premium on your system, click the Show More Choices link and then choose between Best File to File Size (which you specify) and Other Settings (which enables you to select the file size according to the device it's going to be played back on and the rate at which the video data can be sent).

After you're done specifying the vital information for the type of location you select, the wizard saves your movie.

When Windows Movie Maker finishes saving a movie on your hard disk, the wizard automatically plays it in Windows Media Player when you click the Finish button. If you don't want to view the movie right away, click the Play Movie When I Finish check box to remove its check mark before you click the Finish button.

You can then play your movie later in Windows Media Player after you close the Windows Movie Maker by opening the folder where the movie was saved and simply double-clicking the file icon. Doing this opens the movie file in Windows Media Player.

WordPad

WordPad is a kind of "poor man's" Microsoft Word, offering you basic document editing and formatting capabilities and compatibility with documents created with the real Microsoft Word.

Although it's not nearly as full-featured as Microsoft Word, WordPad is certainly head and shoulders above the Notepad text editor, because WordPad enables you to change fonts and attributes and to format the text with justification or bullets. In fact, WordPad is so sophisticated that you can even preview how pages in the document will print. You access this print preview feature by choosing File⇨Print Preview (or by clicking the Print Preview button on the toolbar — the one with the magnifying glass).

Note that WordPad automatically saves documents in Microsoft Rich Text Format (RTF), which can be read by Microsoft Word. WordPad can open only text files or files saved in this RTF file format. To open a Word document with WordPad, you must first save the Word document in RTF format by selecting Rich Text Format as the file type in the Save As Type drop-down list box in the Word Save As dialog box.

Part IV

The Windows Control Panel

The Windows Control Panel contains a bunch of little specialized utility programs designed to make it easy for you to customize your computer. In Windows XP, Control Panel options are now organized into related categories. When you select one of these categories in the Control Panel window, a new window appears, offering you links for viewing and changing particular settings related to that category.

In this part . . .

About the Control Panel

The Control Panel in Windows XP is the place to go when you need to make changes to various settings of your computer system. To open the Control Panel window, click the Start button on the taskbar and then click Control Panel on the Start menu. In Windows XP, you can view the Control Panel in two different views: the Classic View, where the individual Control panel program icons are displayed, and the Category View, where links representing groups of related Control Panel programs are shown. To switch from one view to the other, click the <u>Switch to Classic View</u> link (which appears when you're in Category View) or the <u>Switch to Category View</u> link (which appears when you're in Classic View) at the Control Panel navigation pane.

As you start using Windows, you may find it easier to manage your computer system when the Control Panel is in Category View. The Control Panel window in Category View appears in the following figure.

The Category View of the Control Panel window is organized into 10 categories. To open a window with the Control Panel options for any one of these categories, simply click the category hyperlink.

The next figure shows you how the Control Panel looks in Classic View. When you display the Control Panel in Classic View, Windows displays an alphabetical listing of all the Control Panel options, showing the icon for each, as shown in the following figure. To view and possibly change the settings for a particular Control Panel option, double-click the icon.

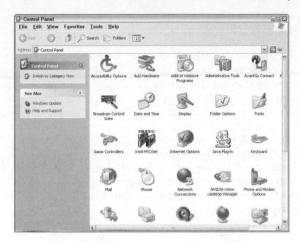

When you first install Windows XP, the Windows installer program checks all of your computer hardware (both internal and external). From this inventory, the installer determines which of the many utilities to add to the various categories of your Control Panel. As a result, your Control Panel may not have all the programs that are showcased in this part of the book (this is especially true if you have a desktop computer, because some of these utilities, such as PC Card, are needed only on notebook computers).

Accessibility Options

When you click the <u>Accessibility Options</u> link when the Control Panel window is in Category View, the Accessibility Options window opens. This window contains the following hyperlink options, the first two under the "Pick a Task" heading and the last one under the "or Pick a Control Panel Icon" heading:

✔ **Adjust the Contrast for Text and Colors on Your Screen:** Displays the Accessibility Options dialog box with the Display tab selected so that you can enable the high-contrast feature to make the screen colors and fonts more legible or so that you can change the blinking rate or the width of the cursor (*see* "Display" in the following list for details).

✔ **Configure Windows to Work for Your Vision, Hearing, and Mobility Needs:** Opens the Accessibility Wizard, which walks you through the steps for configuring an input device other than a mouse or to change how Windows commands are completed.

✔ **Accessibility Options:** Displays the Accessibility Options dialog box, in which you can modify settings for the keyboard, sound, display, and the mouse.

The Accessibility Options dialog box enables you to change a number of keyboard, sound, display, and mouse settings that can make using the computer easier if you have less-than-perfect physical dexterity. The dialog box contains the following five tabs:

✔ **Keyboard:** The Keyboard tab contains three options: Use StickyKeys to have the Shift, Ctrl, and Alt keys remain depressed when you press any of them one time; Use FilterKeys to have Windows ignore repeated keystrokes; and Use ToggleKeys to hear tones when you press the Caps Lock, Num Lock, or Scroll Lock keys.

✔ **Sound:** The Sound tab contains two options: Use SoundSentry to display visual warnings when Windows makes some kind of alert sound; and Use ShowSounds to display captions for the various alert sounds made by the programs that you use.

✔ **Display:** The Display tab contains two options: Use High Contrast to switch to colors and fonts designed to make the screen easier to read; and Cursor Options, which enables you to adjust the Cursor Blink Rate and Cursor Width.

✔ **Mouse:** The Mouse tab contains the MouseKeys options that enable you to control the mouse pointer with the numeric keypad.

✔ **General:** The General tab contains options that enable you to automatically turn off the accessibility options after a set time; notify you when an accessibility feature is turned on or off; and engage the Use Serial Keys option, which lets other special input devices that you've installed on your computer take over for the keyboard and mouse.

Note that many options on the different tabs of the Accessibility Options dialog box have a Settings button that you can select to further refine the option you're activating. The particular settings available vary according to the type of option.

Add or Remove Programs

When you click the <u>Add or Remove Programs</u> link when the Control Panel window is in Category View, the Add or Remove Programs window appears. The Add or Remove Programs window enables you to install or uninstall programs on your computer (*see* "Adding or Removing Programs" in Part I for details).

Appearance and Themes

When you click the <u>Appearance and Themes</u> link when the Control Panel window is in Category View, the Appearance and Themes window opens. This window contains the following hyperlink options (the first four options appear under the heading "Pick a Task," whereas the last three options appear under the heading "or Pick a Control Panel Icon"):

✓ **Change the Computer's Theme:** Opens the Display Properties dialog box with the Themes tab selected. Use the options on this tab to select a new theme that controls the look of your desktop by selecting a background image and windows color scheme. You can also use this tab to control the sounds that are played when different events occur by selecting a particular group of sound icons.

✓ **Change the Desktop Background:** Opens the Display Properties dialog box with the Desktop tab selected so that you can select a new background image for the desktop and icon background color or change which desktop icons and Web items are displayed.

✓ **Choose a Screen Saver:** Opens the Display Properties dialog box with the Screen Save tab selected so that you can select a new screen saver and modify the settings, as well as customize your monitor power settings.

✓ **Change the Screen Resolution:** Opens the Display Properties dialog box with the Setting selected so that you can select a new screen resolution setting or change the color depth (quality).

✓ **Display:** Opens the Display Properties dialog box so that you can customize any display settings, including the computer theme, desktop background, windows color scheme, the Windows screen saver, and the screen resolution; *see* the section "Display" later in this part for more on changing display options.

✓ **Folder Options:** Opens the Folder Options dialog box, where you can customize how folders appear and are accessed within windows, as well as which files are displayed and with what programs they are associated; *see* "Folder Options" that follows immediately for details.

✓ **Taskbar and Start Menu:** Opens the Taskbar and Start Menu Properties dialog box, where you can modify the settings for both the Windows taskbar and the Start menu; *see* "Customizing the taskbar and Start menu" in Part I for details.

Folder Options

When you click the <u>Folder Options</u> hyperlink in the Appearance and Themes window, Windows opens the Folder Options dialog box, which enables you to change the settings for a variety of folder options. The options on the General tab of the Folder Options dialog box enable you to change how you select and open folders in Windows (*see* "Opening Files and Folders" in Part I for more on changing these options).

Use the options on the View tab to designate what types of folders are displayed in windows, such as My Documents, Windows Explorer, and My Computer, and to customize how file and folders are displayed. Use the options on the File Types tab to register new file types. You register a file type by selecting the program that you want Windows to use in opening it. That way, when you double-click a file of that type (indicated by a particular file icon), Windows will launch the registered program (if it's not already running) and then open the selected file within it.

Display

When you click the <u>Display</u> hyperlink in the Appearance and Themes window, you open the Display Properties dialog box, where you're able to customize just about every parameter that affects your monitor display, including the desktop wallpaper, the screen saver, windows color schemes, the number of colors, and the size of the screen area.

Note that in addition to opening the Display Properties dialog box (shown in the following figure) by clicking the <u>Display</u> hyperlink in the Appearance and Themes window, you can open this dialog box by right-clicking somewhere on your Windows desktop and then clicking Properties on the desktop shortcut menu that appears.

The Display Properties dialog box contains the following five tabs:

✔ **Themes:** Assign a new background image and set of desktop icons, along with a new windows color scheme and sound scheme, by selecting that theme in the Theme drop-down list box. To save the current desktop and sound scheme as a new theme, click the Save As button and type a name for the new theme in the File Name text box before clicking the Save button.

✔ **Desktop:** Select a new image for the desktop by selecting that graphics file in the Background list box. To repeat the image as tiles over the entire desktop, click the Position drop-down list button and then click the Tile option on the pop-up menu. To stretch the image so that it occupies the entire screen, click Stretch on this pop-up menu. To change the background color against which the names of desktop icons are displayed, click the Color drop down list button and click the new color in the pop-up color palette. To change which icons are automatically displayed on the desktop, click the Customize Desktop button to open the Desktop Items dialog box and then put a check mark in the check box of each icon to be shown on the General tab. To change which Web items are displayed on the desktop, click the Web tab and then put a check mark in each check box of each Web item to be shown (*see* "Saving Desktop items" in Part II for details on downloading Web items).

✔ **Screen Saver:** Select and configure a screen saver and set the interval after which it kicks in. If you have one of those new energy-saving monitors, you can set the interval after which the monitor goes to lower-power standby or shuts off. On a laptop computer, you can use the Settings button to control the power options, including when the monitor and hard drive power down, as well as when the entire computer goes into standby mode.

✔ **Appearance:** Change the color scheme used by windows and buttons, as well as the font size of the title and option text used in the various windows and dialog boxes. To convert back to the classic (more square and opaque) style of windows and buttons, click the Windows and Buttons drop-down button and then click Windows Classic in the pop-up menu. To select a new color scheme for your window, click the Color Scheme drop-down button and then click the description of the color scheme in the pop-up menu. To select a font size for the windows and dialog box text, click the Font Size drop-down button and then click the new size in the pop-up menu.

✔ **Settings:** Change the color quality between Medium (16 bit) and Highest (32 bit) used by Windows XP, and select a new screen resolution (the higher the number of pixels, the smaller the items and fonts appear on the desktop, enabling Windows to display more stuff on-screen). You can also click the Advanced button to open a dialog box for your monitor in which you can tweak your computer monitor and screen adapter card settings. Click the Troubleshoot button to open a diagnostics screen in the Help and Support Services window that can suggest things to try if you're experiencing screen display problems.

Date, Time, Language, and Regional Options

When you click the <u>Date, Time, Language, and Regional Options</u> link when the Control Panel window is in Category View, the Date, Time, Language, and Regional Options window opens. This window contains the following hyperlink options (the first three are located under the heading "Pick a Task," whereas the last two are under the heading "or Pick a Control Panel Icon"):

✔ **Change the Date and Time:** Opens the Date and Time Properties dialog box with the Date & Time tab selected so that you can update the current date and time. Click the Time Zone tab in this dialog box to select a new time zone for your computer. Click the Internet Time tab to have Windows automatically synchronize the time with a particular Internet time server.

✔ **Change the Format of Numbers, Dates, and Times:** Opens the Regional and Language Options dialog box with the Region Options tab selected so that you can select a new style for displaying numbers, currency, dates, and times in Windows. To select a new style, click the Standards and Formats drop-down button and then click the name of the country whose standards you want to use in the pop-up menu. When you select a new style in this pop-up menu, the styles are then displayed in the text boxes under the heading Samples. To customize a country's standards, click the Customize button and then make changes to individual symbols on the Numbers, Currency, Time, and Date tabs of the Customize Regional Options dialog box. Use the Location drop-down list box to indicate the country in which you're located so that Windows can localize information, such as news and weather, that you receive through the Internet.

✔ **Add Other Languages:** Opens the Regional and Language Options dialog box with the Region Options tab selected so that you can select the Languages tab and then use those options to change the default input language and the methods (Keyboard, Handwriting Recognition, and Voice Recognition) used to input the new language.

✔ **Date and Time:** Opens the Date and Time Properties dialog box with the Date & Time tab selected, just like clicking the <u>Change the Date and Time</u> hyperlink that I describe in a previous bullet.

  ✔ **Regional and Language Options:** Opens the Regional and Language Options dialog box with the Region Options tab selected just like clicking the Change the Formats of Numbers, Dates, and Times hyperlink as I describe in a previous bullet.

Network and Internet Connections

When you click the Network and Internet Connections link when the Control Panel window is in Category View, the Network and Internet Connections window opens. This window contains the following five "Pick a Task" hyperlinks (the other link below represents actual Control Panel icons that do pretty much the same thing):

  ✔ **Set Up or Change Your Internet Connection:** Opens the Internet Properties dialog box with the Connections tab selected. On this tab, you can click the Setup button to open the Internet Connection Wizard (to create a new configuration for logging onto the Internet), or you can click the LAN Settings button (to modify the way your computer is configured to connect with your network).

  ✔ **Create a Connection to the Network at Your Workplace:** Opens the Network Connection Wizard, which takes you through the steps for creating a new dial-up or cable/DSL modem connection to the Internet or VPN (Virtual Private Network) connection for your corporate intranet.

  ✔ **Set Up or Change Your Home or Small Office Network:** Opens the Network Setup Wizard, which takes you through the steps for creating a home or small-business network with which you can share a single Internet connection, as well as all the printers you have connected.

  ✔ **Set Up a Wireless Network for a Home or Small Office:** Opens the Wireless Network Setup Wizard, which walks you through the steps for setting up a network between all your computers with wireless connection points and wireless devices (also known as a wireless infrastructure network).

  ✔ **Change Windows Firewall Settings:** Opens the Windows Firewall dialog box, where you can turn on and off a Windows firewall that protects your computer by preventing unauthorized users from gaining access to its resources over the Internet or through your network. This dialog box contains an Exceptions tab, where you can add or remove programs and services from the exceptions list (a program on this list is able to penetrate the Windows firewall and thus is enabled to send and receive online data, thus increasing the security risk to your system).

Performance and Maintenance

When you click the <u>Performance and Maintenance</u> link when the Control Panel window is in Category View, the Performance and Maintenance window opens. This window contains the following nine hyperlinks for tuning up and maintaining your computer system (the first five appear under the heading "Pick a Task," whereas the following four appear under the heading "or Pick a Control Panel icon"):

✔ **See Basic Information about Your Computer:** Opens the Systems Properties dialog box, which enables you to review and change many system settings for your computer:

- The *General tab* gives you information on versions of Windows XP; the entity to whom the computer is registered; and the processor, speed, and RAM memory of the computer.

- The *Computer Name* tab enables you to change the name of the computer and modify the network ID and domain affiliation.

- The *Hardware* tab enables you to add new hardware and review the device and hardware profiles of your system.

- The *System Restore* tab enables you to turn on and off the System Restore feature and determine how much disk space to allot to it.

- The *Automatic Updates* tab enables you to turn off automatic updates or have Windows notify you when updates are ready to be downloaded and are ready to install.

- The *Remote* tab enables you to turn on and off the Remote Assistance or Remote Desktop features.

- The *Advanced* tab enables you to modify the Performance settings; review the user profiles; and change the system startup, failure, and debugging information on the computer.

✔ **Adjust Visual Effects:** Opens the Performance Options dialog box, where you can select which visual effects to use in Windows. By removing check marks from individual visual-effects check boxes in the Visual Effects list box, you boost the performance of Windows XP. To have Windows select or deselect these options to give you the best performance, click the Best Performance button. To have Windows configure these options for the best appearance, click the Best Appearance button instead. To restore the default settings for these options, click the Restore Defaults button.

✔ **Free Up Space on Your Hard Disk:** Opens the Select Drive dialog box, where you select the drive on which you need to free space. After designating the drive in the Drives drop-down list box, click OK to have Windows check the designated drive to determine which files can be eliminated. Select the files you want removed in the Disk Cleanup dialog box by putting check marks in their check boxes, and click OK to do the disk cleanup.

✔ **Back Up Your Data:** Opens the Backup or Restore Wizard, which you can use both to back up essential files on your computer and to restore files from a previous backup. You can also use this wizard to prepare an Automated System Recovery backup disk, which you can use to reboot your system in the event of a major system failure or computer crash that prevents Windows XP from restarting your computer.

✔ **Rearrange Items on Your Hard Disk to Make Programs Run Faster:** Opens the Disk Defragmenter dialog box, which you can use to both analyze a drive on your computer and, if necessary, defragment the files (by rearranging files so that they're all as contiguous as possible, taking up less disk space and requiring less time to access).

✔ **Administrative Tools** (XP Professional only): Opens the Administrative Tools window, which contains shortcuts to a number of utilities used by the Systems Administrator to review and control your computer. *Note:* You must have System Administrator privileges in order to use any of these utilities.

✔ **Scheduled Tasks:** Opens the Scheduled Tasks window, where you can add, schedule, or run routine maintenance tasks on your computer system; *see* "Scheduled Tasks" in Part III for details.

✔ **Power Options:** Opens the Power Options Properties dialog box, where you create or edit a power scheme that determines when and if Windows should turn off your monitor or power down your hard drive after so many minutes of inactivity. You can also use the controls on the Hibernate tab of this dialog box to enable or disable the hibernation feature, wherein your computer stores whatever programs and files are in memory on the hard drive prior to shutting down (*see* "Shutting Down Windows" in Part I for details). When you restart your computer from hibernation, it returns the system to its previous state upon startup.

✔ **System:** Opens the System Properties dialog box, the same as when you select the <u>See Basic Information about Your Computer</u> link that I describe earlier in this list.

Printers and Other Hardware

When you click the <u>Printers and Other Hardware</u> link when the Control Panel window is in Category View, the Printers and Other Hardware window opens. This window contains the following eight hyperlinks that you can click to modify the printers and hardware you have connected to your system (the first two of which appear under the heading "Pick a Task," while the other six appear under the heading "or Pick a Control Panel Icon"):

✓ **View Installed Printers or Fax Printers:** Opens the Printers and Faxes windows, where you can view and modify existing printers and fax printers.

✓ **Add a Printer:** Opens the Add Printer Wizard, where you can install a new printer on your systems; *see* "Installing a new printer" in Part I for details.

✓ **Game Controllers:** Opens the Game Controllers dialog box, which enables you to review or add game control devices for use with your computer.

✓ **Mouse:** Opens the Mouse Properties dialog box, in which you can modify the settings for your mouse, including switching the primary and secondary buttons, changing the double-click speed, and selecting new pointer icons and pointer movement options for the mouse. If your mouse has a wheel, you can also modify the behavior of rolling the wheel one notch.

✓ **Printers and Faxes:** Opens the Printers and Faxes window, which shows you all of the printers and faxes installed on your computer (same as selecting the <u>View Installed Printers or Fax Printers</u> link that I describe earlier in this list).

✓ **Keyboard:** Opens the Keyboard Properties dialog box, where you can modify the repeat delay and repeat rate for your keyboard and control how fast the cursor blinks.

✓ **Phone and Modem Options:** Opens the Phones and Modem Options dialog box, where you can edit the dialing rules for your location, view and edit the settings for the modems connected to the computer or add a new modem, and view or add new telephony providers.

✓ **Scanners and Cameras:** Opens the Scanners and Cameras window, which enables you to review and add new digital scanners and cameras that you connect to your computer.

Security Center

When you click the <u>Security Center</u> link when the Control Panel window is Category View, Windows opens the Windows Security Center dialog box. Here, you can turn on and off (definitely not recommended) the Firewall, Automatic Updates, and Virus Protection options for your computer, as well as manage the Internet security settings, Automatic Updates (**see** "Using Windows Automatic Update" in Part I), and Windows firewall (including adding programs and services to its exceptions list; **see** "Network and Internet Connections" in this part).

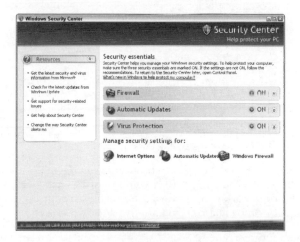

 The Security Center dialog box contains some very important links in the Resources section on the left side. Click the <u>Get the Latest Security and Virus Information from Microsoft</u> link to go online to the Microsoft Security Web page, read the latest security and virus bulletins, and download important security updates for Windows XP. Click the <u>Change the Way Security Center Alerts Me</u> link to make sure that Windows alerts immediately whenever your firewall, automatic updates, and virus protection settings put your system at a definite security risk.

Sounds, Speech, and Audio Devices

When you click the <u>Sounds, Speech, and Audio Devices</u> link when the Control Panel window is in Category View, the Sounds, Speech, and Audio Devices window appears, with the following five hyperlinks for controlling the audio settings on your computer (the first three of which appear under the heading "Pick a Task" and the other two appearing under the heading "or Pick a Control Panel Icon"):

✓ **Adjust the System Volume:** Opens the Sounds and Audio Devices Properties dialog box with the Volume tab selected so that you can adjust the volume or mute the overall volume of your speakers.

✓ **Change the Sound Scheme:** Opens the Sounds and Audio Devices Properties dialog box with the Sounds tab selected so that you can modify or create a new sound scheme that determines what sound, if any, to play when particular events take place, such as closing programs, displaying an alert box, receiving new e-mail, emptying the Recycle Bin, and so on.

✓ **Change the Speaker Settings:** Opens the Sounds and Audio Devices Properties dialog box with the Volume tab selected so that you can use the Speaker Volume button near the bottom to independently adjust the volume for the left and right speakers.

✓ **Sounds and Audio Devices:** Opens the Sounds and Audio Devices Properties dialog box with the Volume tab selected so that you can use the Sounds, Audio, and Voice tabs to modify your computer's audio settings.

✓ **Speech:** Opens the Speech Properties dialog box, where you can modify the Speech Recognition settings used by the Office XP programs, such as Word 2003, if you have this newest version of Office installed, and the Text to Speech settings used by Excel 2003, if you have this version of Excel installed.

User Accounts

When you click the U̲s̲e̲r̲ ̲A̲c̲c̲o̲u̲n̲t̲s̲ link when the Control Panel window is in Category View, the User Accounts window appears, in which you can add and change the properties for the different users on your computer. If you're running Windows XP Professional connected to a corporate network, the User Accounts dialog box appears, in which you can change these settings.

The User Accounts dialog box contains the three hyperlinks C̲h̲a̲n̲g̲e̲ ̲a̲n̲ ̲A̲c̲c̲o̲u̲n̲t̲, C̲r̲e̲a̲t̲e̲ ̲a̲ ̲N̲e̲w̲ ̲A̲c̲c̲o̲u̲n̲t̲, and C̲h̲a̲n̲g̲e̲ ̲M̲y̲ ̲P̲i̲c̲t̲u̲r̲e̲ under the heading "Pick a Task." In addition, M̲a̲i̲l̲ and U̲s̲e̲r̲ ̲A̲c̲c̲o̲u̲n̲t̲s̲ links are listed below under the heading "or Pick a Control Panel Icon."

You use the three "Pick a Task" links to create or modify a user account as follows:

✓ **Change an Account:** Use this option to change the settings for an existing user — including the user name, password, picture

associated with the account, and account type — and change
your .NET Passport account (*see* "Instant messaging" in Part II
for information on how to get a Passport account when signing
up for Windows Messenger). When you click the Change an
Account link, a screen containing the names and pictures for all
the existing accounts appears. To change the settings for a particular account, click the account on this screen to open a new
screen with a list of links to the various settings you can
change. (You can also open this screen by double-clicking the
account name or picture as it appears under the "or Pick an
Account to Change" heading in the initial User Accounts
screen.) To change particular settings, click their links and then
make the appropriate changes on the screen that then appears.
Note that when using the Change My Picture link to select a
new picture to represent your account, you don't have to select
among the ready icons, like the rubber ducky and butterfly. You
can also select one of your own images by clicking the Browse
for More Pictures link and then double-clicking an image in your
My Pictures folder. You also use this option to delete accounts
for users who no longer share your computer by clicking the
Change an Account link.

✔ **Create a New Account:** Use this option to set up an account for
a new user on your computer. When you click the Create a New
Account link, Windows takes you through a set of two screens:
Name the New Account, where you enter the name for the
account, and Pick an Account Type, where you select between
two possible account types. Computer Administrator gives you
permission to add or remove accounts, install programs, access
all files, and make systemwide changes. Limited gives you permission to change your password and picture and to access all
of your files and files in the Shared Documents folder. When you
finish creating a new account by clicking the Create Account
button in the Pick an Account Type screen, Windows randomly
selects a picture for the account and adds it to the initial screen
in the User Accounts window. You can then change the picture
assigned to the account by modifying the new account, using
the Change an Account link as described in the previous bullet
point.

✔ **Change My Picture:** Use this option to select a new graphic
image to represent your user account on the Windows XP
Welcome screen. You can select among the stock images displayed in the User Accounts dialog box or click the Browse for
More Pictures link and select a graphic image in one of the folders on your computer (Windows selects the My Pictures folder
by default).

You can use the two links in the "Or Pick a Control Panel Icon" section to modify any of the following settings:

✔ **Mail:** To open the Mail Setup dialog box for your default e-mail program (Outlook Express or Outlook 2003, in most cases), where you can modify existing e-mail accounts or set up new accounts and change the program's data file and profile settings.

✔ **User Accounts:** To open a second User Accounts window containing a <u>Change the Way Users Log On or Off</u> link in the "Pick a Task" area, followed by icons for the individual user accounts on your computer in the "Or Pick an Account to Change" area. Click a user's icon to change his or her user name, password, picture, or account type. Click the <u>Change the Way Users Log On or Off</u> link to select between the classic logon screen, which prompts you for your user name and password in two separate text boxes, and the new Welcome screen, which enables you to log on simply by clicking your account icon as displayed in the initial Windows screen and then entering your password. To enable the Welcome screen logon method, put a checkmark in the Use the Welcome Screen check box. To use the classic logon, remove the checkmark from this check box. Note that when the Use the Welcome Screen check box contains a checkmark, the Use Fast User Switching check box becomes active (this box is dimmed when the Use the Welcome Screen check box is empty). Click the Use Fast User Switching check box to put a checkmark in it when you want to be able to quickly switch between computer users without having to first close any open programs.

Glossary: Tech Talk

accessories: Tiny (by Microsoft standards) auxiliary programs invented for Windows XP that aren't really necessary to run your computer but can be really handy.

applications: A techie way of saying "programs" — you know, the things that make your computer run around the room and jump through hoops.

browsing offline: *See* work offline.

Clipboard: The place in your system memory where items you want to cut or copy from one place to another are stored. The Clipboard holds only one item at a time, and you can see the current Clipboard contents by using the Clipboard Viewer accessory.

context menu: *See* shortcut menu.

Control menu: A pull-down menu attached to every window in Windows XP that contains the same old tired commands, which you use to resize, relocate, or close the window (just in case you can't adapt to the way Windows XP performs these functions, or you really miss this feature from Windows 3.1). The Control menu appears as a small version of the program's icon in the top left corner of the program's window.

Control Panel: A window full of icons that enables you to customize the many Windows XP settings available for your computer (*see* Part IV).

desktop: The basic background for the Windows XP environment that contains the taskbar and shortcuts to programs and files that you use. The desktop is the place from which you start and end your work session with a Windows computer.

desktop Item: Any World Wide Web component placed directly on your desktop for easy access. Desktop Items (also known as Web items) can include special miniviews of Web pages (such as the MSN stock ticker), actual Web pages, or special applets (such as the 3D Java clock). The contents of desktop items can be routinely synchronized (updated) on a schedule of your choosing.

dialog box: A special, limited type of window that contains any number of buttons, boxes, tabs, and sliders, which you use to specify a whole bunch of settings all at once in Windows XP or in any other particular Windows program you have open.

DOS: An acronym for (choose one) Disk, Damned, Diabolical, Dumb (my favorite) Operating System. DOS is most irrelevant with the advent of Windows XP. You can, however, open a command window with an old-fashioned DOS prompt within Windows XP if you really miss that kind of stuff!

e-mail: Electronic mail. You send and receive e-mail in Windows XP with Outlook Express 6 (*see* Part II for details).

filename: The name you give your files, silly. I'm only bringing it up here because Windows XP allows users to name their files and folders with up to 255 characters, including spaces. Imagine that.

firewall: A system designed to prevent unauthorized access to your computer system through the Internet or a network to which it is connected. A firewall can be implemented through hardware or software or a combination of the two. Service Pack 2 of Windows XP implements a software form of firewall that blocks all suspect data entering or leaving the system (*see* "Security Center" in Part IV).

folder: A data container that holds files, other folders, or a combination of the two. Folders used to be called *directories,* even though their icons looked like folders.

HTML (HyperText Markup Language): The traditional computer programming language for the Web (traditional since 1989 – 1990, when the World Wide Web and HTML language first began to make themselves a presence in the world). HTML can run on almost any computer platform and can combine text with pictures, sounds, and other multimedia enhancements.

HTML document: *See Web page.*

hyperlink: Text or graphics images that you click with the mouse to take you to a certain Web destination (or, rather, have that Web destination appear in your browser window). You can spot a hyperlink when the mouse pointer changes to an outline of a hand. Also, words or other text hyperlinks are almost always underlined text and in blue — which, after you follow the link, changes to purple.

hypertext: Text to which a hyperlink is attached.

icon: A small picture used in Windows XP to make your computer a more GUI (*gooey,* as in *Graphical User Interface*) place to be. Icons identify all manner of objects associated with your computer.

instant messenging: The ability to chat and send messages with all the people that you designate as your contacts. In Windows XP, you do instant messenging with the Windows Messenger software. This program lets you know when any of your contacts come online so that you can engage them in a chat. It also keeps you updated of any change in their status or when they're no longer available (that is, online) for instant communication.

Internet: A large number of computers of all types all hooked together all around the World. The popular multimedia part of the Internet is the World Wide Web.

Internet Explorer: The Microsoft Web browser that connects you to the Internet and enables you to browse the Web pages on the World Wide Web (*see Web browser*). Internet Explorer also opens files on the same computer on which it's running and displays the local files as Web files.

intranet: A small-scale version of the Internet that works the same way as the Internet, but only the authorized members of the corporation or organization that sponsors the intranet get to use it.

MSN Explorer: The MSN version of the Internet browser that logs you onto the Microsoft Network (*see* next entry) and takes you to a customized version of the MSN home page with local weather, news, and links to all your favorite Web sites and online communities.

multimedia: Yeah! It's what we want: music, color, sound — all the stuff that separates the World Wide Web from just plain text on a monochromatic screen. You can experience all sorts of sounds and images with a properly equipped multimedia computer. Much of the popularity of the Web is based on the visual and audio impact of multimedia.

properties: A description of the settings of any object in Windows XP that is represented by an icon. Properties are found in special dialog boxes that you access through the object shortcut menu.

Recycle Bin: The trash can of Windows XP, where you can drag the files, directories, and other stuff that you want to get rid of. Somebody at Microsoft was positively gushing with political correctness when he or she named this thing, because nobody is going to drive up, take the stuff you throw away, and make something wonderful and new with it.

ScreenTips: Windows XP extensively uses ScreenTips to provide a way of adding commentary or footnotes to features. When you run your mouse pointer over a certain part of the screen, a little black-outlined, pale-yellow rectangle pops up with some more or less informative text. In some cases, such as with some Internet search results, this text can amount to a paragraph's worth of context-sensitive material.

shortcut: A remarkable way in Windows XP to open a favorite document, folder, Web page, or program directly from the desktop of your computer without needing to know the real whereabouts.

shortcut menu: A pull-down menu containing commands that relate directly to the object to which they're attached. Shortcut menus can be found almost everywhere in Windows XP. They're attached to program, folder, or file icons, toolbar buttons, open windows, and even the desktop itself. To open a shortcut menu, right-click the object in question with the mouse. Sometimes known as a *context menu.*

Start menu: The mother of all pull-down menus in Windows XP. Located by clicking the ever-present Start button on the taskbar, it contains almost all the commands you'll ever need to use.

taskbar: A bar that contains buttons for opening the Start menu and switching between programs and windows that are currently in use.

toolbar: A bar containing a row of buttons that perform many of the routine tasks you used to have to do with pull-down menus or keystroke combinations in "the old days."

View menu: Located in the menu bar, the View menu enables you to modify in various ways the look and feel of all those icons that are going forth and multiplying in your windows.

Web browser: A program, such as Microsoft Internet Explorer 6, MSN Explorer, or Netscape Navigator, which enables the user or client to visit various Web sites and experience the content found there.

Web page: The basic display unit of the World Wide Web: When you see something on the Internet, it is most likely a Web page. The Web page itself may be composed of a number of parts, including the HTML source and various multimedia images.

window: The basic on-screen box used in Windows XP to contain and display each and every program you run on your computer.

Windows Messenger: The name of the instant messaging program in Windows XP that enables you to keep in constant contact with people on your contact list. The latest version of Windows Messenger enables you to send file and photos and even share applications across the Internet.

wizards: A particular set of dialog boxes used in Windows XP and other Microsoft products to step the user through complex procedures, such as installing a new printer, sending a fax, or performing coronary angioplasty.

work offline: When you aren't connected to the Internet and you use a browser (like Internet Explorer 6) to browse Web pages or e-mail and newsgroup messages that have been downloaded onto your own computer, you're working offline. With the advent of Web channels and Web page subscriptions, you can have new content automatically downloaded during the wee hours of the night, when you're not bothered by Internet traffic and lengthy downloads. You can then view the downloads offline at your leisure.

XML: (Extensible MarkUp Language) Like its cousin, HTML (HyperText Markup Language that renders Web pages on the Internet) XML is a markup language that uses codes called tags to define the documents structure and appearance. Unlike HTML, whose tags are all predefined and set in stone (at least until a new version comes out), XML is extensible in the sense that you (well, actually not you, but a trained programmer) can define and create new tags as needed as needed for any particular project. Also unlike XML actually describes the structure and meaning of its data whereas HTML only defines how its data looks (and beauty, as they say, is only skin-deep). It is this latter quality that makes XML so valuable in terms of sharing data among different incompatible systems, making it easy to reuse the data wherever it's needed.

Index

Notes

Notes

Notes